Sam,
        Thank y[...]
May you have [...]
encouragement within these
pages. Stay open and be
blessed.
                    peace,
                    Deongah Gregg 19

Printed in the United States of America

ISBN 978-0-692-66946-4 (paperback)
ISBN 978-0-692-66947-1 (eBook)

Dorothy Jean Publishing, LLC
P.O. Box 248574
Columbus, OH 43224

Cover Design by Marshall L. Shorts, ARTfluential

Author's Photo by Toy L. Okotete

Falling Into Faith:
The Source Of My Power

A Memoir

DeAngelo Griggs

DOROTHY
JEAN
PUBLISHING

I learned this, at least, by my experiment:
that if one advances confidently
in the direction of his dreams, and endeavors
to live the life which he has imagined,
he will meet with a success unexpected in common
hours.
He will put some things behind,
will pass an invisible boundary;
new, universal, and more liberal laws
will begin to establish themselves around and within
him;
or the old laws be expanded,
and interpreted in his favor in a more liberal sense,
and he will live with the license of a higher order of
beings.
In proportion as he simplifies his life,
the laws of the universe will appear less complex,
and solitude will not be solitude,
nor poverty poverty,
nor weakness weakness.
If you have built castles in the air,
your work need not be lost;
that is where they should be.
Now put the foundations under them.

- Henry David Thoreau

To Cape Town, with Love!

CONTENTS

PREFACE

I'm not exactly sure what moved me to write about my experiences. Perhaps I felt the need to record what was going on to find out exactly what happened. In just a few weeks' time, the life I'd once known—the life I'd planned—was gone. It's hard for me to put into words the exact feeling that came across my mind at that exact moment, but when I say I had to fight for my life—my biggest enemy was not He, but me. You never realize how important life is until you're on the verge of losing it. My life, the one I'd known, was over in a South African hospital with the words, "You have cancer in your blood." Writing is expressive for me; it's a therapeutic journey that has allowed me to share my physical and emotional pain.

I began to study philosophical principles and social concepts from notable thinkers such as Michel de Montaigne, whose essay *That to Study Philosophy is to Learn to Die* affected my perception of death when I first read it. Dr. Cornell West's views on cultivating seeds of knowledge in my people allowed me to see how one person can have a profound impact on another's life. There were a few other scholars who helped set the foundations and preparations for my battle, as my spirituality took on new elements. I discovered broad and diverse principles that later proved to help me live a more fulfilling life. These spiritual teachings range from scriptures of the Holy Bible to verses of the Bhagavad-Gita[1] and other enlightening principles. In addition, daily prayers and meditation became effective tools and weapons of strength to help me cope with and have hope in the reality of my life-threatening illness and the difficult journey to survive.

In the midst of learning and applying philosophical and spiritual principles, I nurtured from within the strength and courage to open myself up to the idea of love. Not the type of love present in the physical attraction to another human being—rather, a love deriving from kindness, compassion, peace, hope and empathy toward other beings. These virtues, I believe, are necessary to experience the fullness of life and the best it has to offer. Such virtues also inspired me to give my very best *to* life.

It was important to me to be as open as possible while

---

[1] Bhagavad-Gita: The Bhagavad-Gita is the eternal message of spiritual wisdom from ancient India. The word Gita means song and the word Bhagavad means God, often the Bhagavad-Gita is called the Song of God. (http://www.bhagavad-gita.org/Articles/faq.html).

writing this journal. I discovered comfort in conversations, expressing my feelings and emotions to my therapist and eventually my family and friends. There was confession in my unidentifiable emotions that only an expert like my therapist could help me understand. This enabled me to later express the certain lessons I have learned and the knowledge I have gained. This quickly turned into insightful and helpful knowledge—not only for myself, but for family and friends as well. I soon realized that my journey became an inspiration to others, indirectly and unconsciously. At times I questioned myself, asking, "Are my sufferings for others to learn from? Why was I chosen to be the teacher and not the student?" To me, my sufferings were not encouraging, they were painful. These moments of unfairness led to many bouts of anger and, at times, doubt and depression.

One thing is clear: nothing lasts forever. Nothing in life—good or bad—nothing will last. This was the life lesson I needed in order to persevere.

As I entered my late twenties, I had to take a critical inventory of my life. From evaluating my future goals and balancing my newfound illness, it was a journey destined for me to live. I had graduated from Miami University of Ohio with a degree in Marketing, and moved to Columbus, Ohio from Chicago, Illinois to be with my girlfriend of two years. I had just spent my second week of a six-week volunteer experience in Cape Town, South Africa, where I served as a teacher's aide to fifth and sixth grade children at a township school. I had invested time and research on how to live a more enlightened and productive life, simply trying to live by the Golden Rule of treating others with love, kindness and compassion, as I would want to be treated. I was trying to live an in-the-moment life and not consume myself with the past or future, really occupying a present space in a world filled with so many distractions. I had no idea my findings would include a cancer diagnosis during an emergency visit to a Cape Town hospital.

PART ONE: LIFE-CHANGING EXPERIENCE

I could hardly stand straight. My legs felt weak and I was extremely fatigued. The looks on people's faces surrounded me, each one expressing more concern than the last. It was as if they were looking at someone on his very last breath, which was ironic, because that is exactly how I felt. Before I knew it, I was being rushed to the hospital where the battle of a lifetime awaited me. Ultimately, this would save my life, because on April 17, 2011, I, DeAngelo Griggs, was diagnosed with Acute Lymphoblastic Leukemia.

How did a life-changing experience turn into a life-changing nightmare? How do I even begin to answer the question everyone's going to ask me? You know, the one question most people will ask to be polite: "How was your volunteer trip to Cape Town, South Africa?" Should I put it politely or be brutally honest? Because any normal human being would say, "It was literally a life-changing experience and I learned a lot about myself. How's your internship going?" I'm still being truthful, right? Let's try this again, but this time me being brutally honest: "It was scary, painful and the worst experience I have ever had. Oh, and guess what? I

1

brought back this little souvenir called cancer. Don't worry, it's not contagious. How's your summer going?"

My subtle humor isn't very funny, is it? I didn't think so. I might go on and say, "It's not you, it's me," and apologize, because being terminally ill puts me in a bad mood and I'm actually a decent person. Then they might feel bad and say, "It's okay. Why do bad things happen to good people?" And I might just sit there and nod as they tell me how sorry they feel for me. That's what it's like when you have cancer. People feel bad for you, even when they don't have to. They really don't need to, either, because I feel plenty bad for the both of us.

However, being stricken with leukemia reinforced what I have always known: the healing power of prayer and faith. Before I was diagnosed, I'd begun to refocus my life on getting closer to God. I had fallen into a terrible cycle where I'd stopped talking with God and started talking to God, as if I could fully understand His immense powers. I would find prayers online and lock them in my smart phone to read conveniently, in the hopes they would change my life. I was a microwave person, the type of person who gives a demand with the expectations of an immediate return, just like a bag of popcorn—after two to three minutes of cooking, I could satisfy my cravings. This was who I was when it came to asking God for materialistic things. Quite frankly, if it weren't for being diagnosed with leukemia, I would undoubtedly still be microwave-wishing!

***

My transformations began to take place a few months prior to my diagnosis, in January of 2011. I had travelled to Cleveland, Ohio to attend my best friends' baby shower with my girlfriend, Toy. The night before the baby shower, at another friend's house, we sat around socializing after a few of us had been out drinking. We conversed about various aspects of life. I knew I was intoxicated, and conventional wisdom should have taught me to go to bed for the night. At the time, however, I wasn't operating in a conventional state of mind, nor did I have much wisdom. I am not even sure how the debate started. All I know is the topic was religion. This was when my life as I knew it started to transform.

I have learned since that I am no expert on subjects I once arrogantly claimed to know. With regard to religion and God's intentions especially, I thought I knew it all. On this particular night, I expressed my disappointment in religion and God, despite some of my friends' personal testimonies, which I had a front row seat to witness.

Their spiritual journey did not apply to me, but deep

inside I envied and hated what I was craving: God's grace. I wanted the favor of God in my life, and His presence was nowhere to be seen as far as I was concerned. I expressed a lot of anger that night with words that no doubt offended my friends. By the time I did make it to the guestroom, I was disappointed with myself for speaking against what I truly believed, that God is real. I could recall countless times I had overcome life obstacles only through the grace of God. The disappointment felt familiar to me. It would come after I believed I could trump God in some shape or form. It did not matter if I discussed it with one person or an entire group. The disappointment weighed heavily on me, heavier than anything I could clearly describe, and it never went away immediately. Worst of all, I brought it on myself. For brief moments, I would psych myself out by thinking I was fine, but to be honest my soul was deteriorating and I was destroying my path to the peace of mind I needed.

It was odd, the way I questioned God. I knew God was real because of the miracles I witnessed every day in many people's lives close to me. But it was hard for me to trust in Him. All of my opportunities and resources were from the mercy and grace of God, but I did not know how to be truly grateful for them yet.

The rest of the weekend felt cold—and I am not talking

about the harsh temperatures normally present during the winter months of the Midwest. I felt cold in the sense of being numb to anyone and everything around me, even in the midst of the baby shower. My best friend's son was on his way into the world, and here I was, sulking in my own misery. I was there physically, in the middle of the festivities, and I loved seeing my best friend and his wife receive so much love. Yet my actions from the previous night had planted themselves uncomfortably in my conscious mind, and I felt so insecure. I truly thought people could see right through me, thinking that all the positivity and hope I encouraged in others was only talk and I didn't truly mean it. It was as if I was a fraud and had finally been exposed for not being real and authentic. It seemed like my entire life so far had been this "big pretend," and now everyone else knew.

Several days following the baby shower, my best friend called to express his concern about my spirited comments during my visit. He could tell by my tone that I was desperate for religious answers. He was right. He explained that while I had been adamant about proving my point the other night, I had not recognized that I had given his wife a new perspective on the story of Job. The Book of Job was my go-to story in response to whoever tried to explain the love and compassion of God.

My thought process was this: If God was so loving and compassionate to His people, why would he jeopardize his faithful servant Job's livelihood? At the time, however, I had only ever read up until the point of where Job's first set of children died. As far as I was concerned, no loving and compassionate God would do such a thing to a person as good-hearted and cheerful-spirited as Job. In the beginning of the story, Satan receives permission from God to inflict danger and ill will on Job, in an attempt to make Job curse God. This ultimately leads to Job's faith being tested in the most extreme conditions. I could not understand God's "compassion" and I refused to accept it.

My best friend is a dear brother indeed. He has always held me accountable for my actions, especially for my verbal actions. And I do the same for him whenever necessary. I have a very close group of friends and we all keep each other accountable for our actions. Whether we, as individuals, decide to take the advice and make better choices is simply up to that individual. I love and respect these men and consider them very strong and knowledgeable people. Despite my personal inner demons and struggles, I admire their progress and tenacity to always do better for themselves and their families.

***

Around February, I woke up in the middle of night sweating like I had played at least three games of recreational basketball. During the following weeks, I blew it off as a common cold symptom and didn't think much more of it. However, I didn't have a cough, stuffy nose or any sneezing. I figured over-the-counter cold medications would make me feel better before it got worse. But the night sweats persisted even after another week went by. My next assumption was that Toy and I needed a new mattress. At the time, I was working at a major retail store in the furniture department, and I had learned more information about mattresses with latex layers that kept the body cool at night versus memory foam, which retained heat. Our mattress was old, with a memory foam core. That had to be the problem, I thought. With no money to spare and a major trip to Africa approaching, a new mattress purchase was not part of the equation.

As time went on, I made some adjustments to my sleeping pattern, like sleeping near the window and turning on the fan, as well as removing layers of clothing and blankets. This made a small difference, but the night sweats were still unusual. Suddenly, I began to notice my appetite diminishing and the waistline on some of my pants enlarging.

I realized that my pants weren't growing; I was losing weight. I attributed the weight loss to my lack of eating, so somehow I could make sense of the sudden, unexplained changes in my body. I remember Toy and I eating at a restaurant the night before it got really bad. At this particular restaurant I normally ordered wings, salad and a beer. I remember eating two forkfuls of the salad and maybe two wings before I could no longer eat. Soon after, my legs began to shake feverously. I thought it was anxiety, but that didn't really make sense. I recall the look of concern on Toy's face when she saw how bad I felt. She looked sad and disappointed for the simple fact there was nothing she could do to ease my pain. She looked helpless; the burden to "fix" me weighed heavily, evident by her facial expressions. She desperately wanted to know what was bothering me, but I didn't have an answer. I had no clue what was happening to me.

Later that evening, Toy consoled me and gave me a sound peace of mind. Her words of encouragement comforted me and eliminated all preconceived thoughts or . worries. She spoke about our volunteer trip to South Africa and how our lives were moving in a positive direction. She said, "God will take care of everything." But something terrible was happening to me. It was bothering me physically, mentally and spiritually. My soul was in trouble. A voice from within advised me to get back to a place of worship. My mind, body and soul needed to get closer to God as quickly as possible. Despite the many animosities I had toward God, this particular voice told me to get to church, get on my knees and pray. I can't tell you if it was premonition or fear; all I knew was that my life was about to change. I knew I needed God's guidance and I went back to church. I remember boasting to everyone how I was attending church again and giving God a second chance. It's beyond laughable to me now, when I recall how arrogant this comment was. I was going to give *God* a second chance? Honestly, who was I? I would soon learn who was in charge and who held the tryouts.

The best part of church service was listening to the preacher or priest speak about the word of God. It was intriguing and thought provoking how they could relate the sermon to everyday life. Attending church always made me feel better about the upcoming week—something about a fresh start or new beginning, I suppose.

In my approach to re-entering church—and I do mean "re-entering"—I decided to go on my own terms. I told myself I would go to great lengths to personally dissect whatever messages from the Bible and sermon were offered.

I was convinced I could take the word and basically rewrite it to fit my own personal lifestyle. To be honest, these false beliefs gave me great satisfaction. I achieved this idea of believing *I* was the one in total control—but I wasn't. A one-way ticket to an untold destination was on its way; and unfortunately, I was riding first class.

***

The evening before I went to the emergency room, I was at work. Surprisingly, during my dinner break, I had a small appetite and was able to eat a full personal pizza. When I got back on the sales floor, my chest began to hurt. At first, I thought it was heartburn, but then my legs felt a striking pain. A pain that hurt so bad, I could barely walk for more than three minutes. I told my co-worker I was going to sit down in the hopes of subsiding the pain from my legs. After about three or five minutes, I got up to walk again. Within twenty seconds, the pain was back. It ran down the back of my waist, from my legs to my knees. I stood stationary for a moment, and my knees begin to buckle. I grabbed the nearest chair and sat down.

I started thinking about this awkward pain I felt. The chest pain, I was convinced, was nothing more than heartburn. At the very least, I thought, other than heartburn, it could be food poisoning, which would be no big deal. Heartburn was nothing more than taking a few antacids, I justified once more.

As I continued sitting, the pain in my legs became intolerable. Had I lifted something heavy? Was it a hernia? Maybe Father Time had kicked off his shoes and joined me on the sofa without an invitation, even though I was only twenty-seven? Each assumption held a compelling argument. My mind became more and more preoccupied with the fate of my health. What in the world was happening to me? That was the million-dollar question that even I didn't have an answer to.

When the time came to clock out, I was more than ready to leave. I called Toy twenty minutes before my shift was over so I could get home sooner. I needed medicine, sleep—just anything to take the pain away. The pain was like nothing I had ever felt before. It was as if someone was repeatedly piercing me through my chest and through the back of my legs with one of the sharpest knives known to man.

It had begun to rain and got very windy outside. It was cold, and the wind smacked against my face. Each time the wind blew, rain would make its way toward me and send chills throughout my body. As I leaned against a light post in the parking garage, my legs started to shake and buckle uncontrollably. I hoped the rain would serve as a distraction for my co-workers exiting the building, so they wouldn't notice my odd behavior. Soon after, Toy arrived. I hurried to the passenger side of the car. When I got in the car, I was trembling and swaying my legs back and forth. I placed my hand on my chest as the pain continued, intensified. All I could do to communicate my discomfort was let out grunt after grunt. From within, I was screaming, "HELP ME!" Sadly, the expression on Toy's face was grave concern.

Toy asked what was wrong, and once again I did not have an answer for her. Soon enough we made it home, but I could barely move. I slipped off my shoes, ripped off my coat and laid on our sofa in the living room. I tried to explain the pain in my chest and legs, but I just wanted antacids and pain medication to ease me into sleep. After an hour or so of lying on the sofa I stood up. I managed to make it to the bedroom, but I was still in bad shape. I tossed in and out of cold sweats for hours, hoping the pain would pass.

Thank God Toy was by my side, because she took complete control of the situation. Toy rolled over to my side of the bed, and without entertaining any more of my, "I'm okay, babe," "Don't worry," and "I just need sleep," responses, she said, "Let's go, I'm taking you to the emergency room right now!" Before I knew it, we were riding down the freeway and I was heading to a place I had been trying to avoid for the longest time: the hospital.

A funny thing about emergency rooms is that when there aren't people there to be treated and you're the only person who needs attention, the wait time seems comparable to being in line at the DMV. The people sitting behind the receptionist desk appeared to have less interest for situations falling under the term "emergency." Then again, it could have just been me. "Excuse me," I said, not caring whose attention I garnered. "I'm in some serious pain, my legs hurt and my chest feels like someone is jabbing a knife in me."

A few minutes later, I was finally called and led back into a Triage room. It must have been close to midnight, and I was the only visible patient in Triage. We walked into a room with white painted walls. A desk stood on the right side with three chairs surrounding it, one for the nurse and the other two for Toy and me. The nurse took my right arm and wrapped it in a blood pressure cuff to check my blood circulation. She then took my temperature using the wall thermometer mounted on the wall above my chair. The nurse was very attentive and did not appear distressed, until I explained my agonizing chest pains. She suddenly had me stand up and walked me outside the room to a bed covered with white sheets. She had me lie down as she diligently prepared me for a heart test using an EKG (Electrocardiogram) machine, placing electrodes on my chest and abdominal areas. I was already nervous from how the nurse had hurried me out of the room to the bed, but being hooked up to the machine intensified my anxiety.

According to the tests, my heart checked out fine, but the nurse said I still needed to see a doctor. I thought the pain was perhaps mental, because for a brief moment I finally felt a sense of relief. The fact that I was in the care of medical professionals eased my mind. The pain in my legs decreased to where I didn't feel the need to massage them for relief. And my chest pain suddenly disappeared, maybe because I no longer felt as anxious and jittery as when I first arrived. I supposed that if I passed out, I was already in the hospital, which gave me a tiny sense of comfort.

After we reviewed my medical information, I was taken into the Intensive Care Unit. As we walked, my chest pain came back and my legs went back into the severe pain, forcing me to limp. Despite the physical pain, it hurt me even more to see the look of worry and uncertainty in Toy's eyes. I had never seen her this worried in all the time we'd been together. She looked frightened, which made me fight harder to be strong for her. Even though I was in severe pain,

I had to be strong not only for her, but for us. Neither of us knew what was going on, and I knew it was killing her that there was nothing she could do to take away the pain. She's a caregiver by nature, but all we could do at that moment was wait. Within those long three hours, I cursed at every wall, at every television commercial and—I am ashamed to admit— at Toy. I needed the pain to subside, but no one in the ICU was helping me. The unbearable pain continued to persist and I was left with my increasing anger.

Toy reassured me that help was on the way, and she too felt angst at the lack of medical attention. As time went by, I was able to focus my mind to block out the pain. For some odd reason, I focused on the hooks that held up the off-white curtains that surrounded my room. They reminded me of the drawings of the Hangman game I used to play growing up. I imagined I was one of them, just hanging onto life by a thread. Suddenly, I heard a guy whose pain may have exceeded my own. He groaned and moaned so loudly that he captured the attention of every nurse in our unit. A woman cried out several times, "SOMEONE, PLEASE HELP HIM!" I looked at Toy as we heard this man's agony, and I said, "It could be far worse for me, huh?" She didn't say a word, but just nodded her head.

Moments later, a doctor and nurse entered my room,

and I went back through the details of my ongoing pains. They gave me some pain medication through an IV, and drew my blood soon after. With a million questions circulating through my mind, I wondered what it could be. From tuberculosis to lupus, my mind wandered in the worst way. Although I questioned it all, I had one particular disease that lurked in the back of my mind, seen as both physically and socially detrimental in today's world: HIV/AIDS.

***

My test results came back a couple of hours later and everything was negative with the exception of contracting Influenza B (Flu B), which was supposed to explain my illness. It was shocking to find out that a mere cold, without coughing or sneezing, could attack my body in such a way. In addition to the Flu B, the scans and X-rays taken of my chest revealed that since birth, the aorta tube in my heart was abnormal. They say the aorta tube typically goes out to the left side of the body, whereas mine goes out to the right. It was nothing to be concerned about; however, I would need to see a heart specialist in the future. I figured that since it had been abnormal since birth and I didn't have any major issues, I was finally going to leave the hospital. The plan was to get the Flu B out of my system and do the appropriate follow up for my heart. This all seemed good to me, until my third set of vitals revealed that my temperature had shot up to 102 degrees, and I was officially admitted into the hospital.

By the time a room was ready for me, it was well into Friday morning. I still hadn't eaten any food since the personal pizza from the previous night at work. Since I would be there for the next day and a half or so, it was decided that my heart be monitored. I was discharged late Saturday afternoon and sent home with flu medication that would last me the next seven to ten days.

I remember, as we left the hospital, expressing to Toy how I had never imagined that a cold could set a person back so far. She quickly reminded me that I had just been diagnosed with the flu, not a cold. There was a world of difference between dealing with the "common cold" and the "flu." I left it alone; all I wanted to do was get back to being me and get back to a life without the pain and discomfort.

***

Two days later, I began to feel a little better. I returned to work, but as the week went on, the pain — particularly in my lower back and down my legs — returned. At this point, I didn't want to go back to the hospital. They'd run all the tests they could, examined my blood work and hospitalized me for two days. I was fine and just had to tough it out.

At the end of the week, one of my co-workers noticed my new stride, or lack thereof, as I walked around the sales floor in pain. She asked what was wrong, and I explained the pain to her. Suddenly, a new seed was planted. She said it sounded like I was experiencing sciatica. I had never heard of sciatica, and of course I was curious. I immediately took out my smart phone and began researching sciatica on the web. Sciatica is the pain in your sciatic nerve that goes through your lower back, buttocks and hips. It travels down the back of your legs causing tingling and numbness, weakening the legs.

My prayers had finally been answered. Nearly every symptom I was experiencing aligned with sciatica. The symptoms detailed the sharp pain in my lower back through my legs and hips. It all made sense, from the difficulty to walk, stand or sit for long periods of time. I started to believe there was a reason for all my pains.

My research on sciatica equipped me with just enough knowledge for me to be dangerous. So my self-diagnosis of this disease should come as no surprise. I wasn't trying to see any more doctors, nurses or hospitals. For the next week or so, I took pain pills, used hot and cold packs, used ace bandages, did leg stretches and leg exercises—and somewhere in between all of this, I even tried yoga.

I was about two and half weeks out before my trip to Africa. I was still very excited to go to Africa, despite feeling weak physically. Even though the mental toil of being sick and in pain was weighing heavily on my mind, my curiosity to see Africa remained strong. I was emotionally invested in going to Africa, and nothing could sway me otherwise. Toy and I had always wanted to travel abroad, and Africa was one of the many travel destinations we wanted to explore. I had always been interested in volunteer work and suggested that we make our trip more productive and enlightening during our stay.

One reason I wanted to go to Africa in particular was because of a conversation I'd had several months prior, with a woman from work who was native to Africa. One day she commented on my facial features, specifically my forehead, and asked if I was African. I told her my paternal grandfather was Nigerian. She asked if I had ever been to Africa and I told her no. She said, "You need to go, because there is where you will find the source of your power!" Obviously, a person doesn't have these sorts of conversations regularly in life, and this really made an impression on me. So much so, in fact, that I believed my life would be incomplete unless I made it to Africa. This woman had planted a seed in me that would soon grow into fruition when Toy presented the idea to travel abroad.

Somewhere between the two and a half weeks before Africa, a new type of pain occurred. It was a dull and irritating sensation in my back, right below my lower shoulder blade. I questioned whether it was from bad posture over recent weeks, but it quickly got worse.

The same co-worker who had talked to me about sciatica gave me her very honest opinion. First of all, she mentioned the discoloration of my skin and asked if the doctors had checked for anemia. She was wiser and older, but more importantly, her understanding about life motivated me to act responsibly. She said, "It's none of my business, but I noticed you haven't been well for several weeks. I know you say you went to the hospital and blood work was done, but I think you should go back and make sure they've checked for it all." I could tell she had my best interest at heart as she continued to express how my health was most important, at all costs. She hit home when she asked me to evaluate and think about Toy and my family. Was it fair that I myself had no clue of what was happening, and they didn't either, and could be suffering as well? Obviously not physically, but mentally and emotionally someone else's livelihood was being affected. I was being prideful by thinking solely of myself.

I wanted to swallow my pride, but I could not bring myself to do it. Instead, I hid my pride and did not let it go, as I should have. I felt cowardly, for not fully letting go. After I thanked my co-worker, I left work to head back to the hospital. On the way, I called Toy and told her where I was heading and insisted I go alone. I told her I would be fine and she took my word for it.

When I arrived at the urgent care, I met with another doctor for a second opinion. I informed him of my flu diagnosis, constant body pains and lack of sleep. After he took my vitals, he diagnosed me with a condition called *Bursitis*. Apparently, this infection is caused by the flu and may cause a residual result. The doctor informed me that I should have been prescribed antibiotics after my first diagnosis. And there we went, trying again. The option of running more blood work was presented, but that would have cost a couple hundred dollars more. With a trip to Africa drawing near, I couldn't afford to spend any more money. I took the doctor's word for truth and left the hospital once more feeling that my situation had been resolved.

Everything was in full motion. I would get the infection out my system and my legs would get better. My appetite would improve and I would sleep at night. More importantly, my conscience would be clear of others worrying about me. With a slow but steady progression, I started to feel like myself again. The pain below my shoulder blade went away. I was able to eat real food again.

It was March 12, 2011, and I woke up happy to simply be alive. Fresh off four hours of sleep, it was my twenty-eighth birthday! Despite everything, this was a day I couldn't help but be thankful for as I celebrated another year of life. It was a Saturday, and I was able to work an early shift; this worked out great, because Toy had planned a dinner for me and invited people out to celebrate with us. I was worn down early in the day, but I tried to keep a positive mindset. I drank energy drinks and took supplements to give me an energy boost. Unfortunately, this instant energy left as fast as it came. I could sense things weren't going to get any better, despite seeing the doctor at the urgent care clinic. I was becoming weak again physically, as my legs tired out and the lack of sleep affected me, thus causing me to be less alert. Still, it was my birthday and Toy had worked hard to get people to come together for dinner. I knew the reason she had planned the dinner was to try to get my spirits up. She wanted me to be around love and in a positive environment. As always, she kept me grounded.

Dinner was great; we had a few friends and family

come out, and Toy got me strawberry shortcake to cap things off. I love a nice slice of strawberry shortcake. Now, don't get me wrong, I would have been grateful for any cake she provided—but there's symbolism behind the strawberry shortcake. My mother always cooks a nice soul food dinner for each of her children on their birthday. She has seven children—five young men, two young ladies—and I'm the oldest of the crew. Along with the dinner, my mother also provides the celebrated birthday child with strawberry shortcake. Despite my low energy level, I was completely overwhelmed with gratitude when the cake was revealed.

At this time in my life, the pressure of being the oldest sibling was immensely challenging. I felt a responsibility to blaze the path of success for my younger siblings and I developed a persona to come across as a strong, self-reliant individual. It ultimately became a hindrance to my growth and maturity. This should not have been, but it was the illusion I'd created and oddly embraced. I tried to demonstrate to everyone that I had life under control. Unfortunately, I did not recognize how ineffective such an endeavor could be—and when I did, it was too late. I only added stress to my life by masking my insecurities. I assumed my family and friends didn't want to know about my vulnerabilities and I didn't believe they would accept those parts of me too. They believed in me and appreciated me, but I couldn't find the means to have the same sentiments for myself.

Weak? Not me. I acted on, believing I would soon be good and no one would notice my declining physique or sudden lack of joy for life I'd once enthusiastically encouraged others to have. And in this mindset, I felt no need for my family and friends to be bothered with my troubles. As the dinner continued, I sat silently, listening to others enjoy themselves. The atmosphere became more festive and I definitely wasn't going to interrupt it. I didn't know what was happening to me, and to speak on it seemed like a waste of time.

I found myself lying in bed later that night with the same leg and back problems I'd had for weeks; except this time, I had one mild headache leading to the next day's hangover. Oh, did I mention I'd had a birthday drink before I got to this moment? Okay, okay, I'd had a few drinks—but it was my birthday, can you really blame me?

***

We scheduled to depart for Cape Town, South Africa on March 25, 2011. The change and abnormities in my body were even more continuous by this time, and my mental state was completely unstable. Toy was deeply concerned and thought our trip to Africa might become a burden on me. She punished herself by thinking she was forcing me to go against my will. I could not have disagreed more; I wanted to go to Africa. This was a dream for me, and my heart was ready to grab hold of this life-changing opportunity.

Nothing in life ever goes planned. With only three days left to leave for Africa, I still wasn't getting any confirmation or feedback from management regarding the leave of absence I had requested. I'd put in my request three months prior; I needed some answers.

Let's just say, I never got my answers, and if I did—I didn't like them. The Wednesday before I left for Africa, I put in my resignation. I had just signed up to do a six-week volunteer trip, and nothing felt better than dedicating my full self to helping others. My obligation was to be a teacher's aide with the program in two weeks. I wanted to gain knowledge and cultural understanding from people who lived a completely different life than me. Resigning from my job was the final step in my commitment to going to Africa.

Despite all the physical and mental grief I put myself through, the goal to get to Africa was never a panic. In reality, other than counting down the days to get there and fundraising, Africa was the realest thing outside of Toy in my life. I put up no less than a fight to have it remain this way, even though there were a few people in my life who had given their own opinions about me not going. I felt a much deeper purpose than the resistant voices around me. I knew my future was connected to Africa—not in a predictive way, but a spiritual one.

The day before we departed, I again suffered through a sleepless and painful night. As soon as the sun was up, I asked Toy to take me back to the emergency room. I was determined for them to prescribe a new medication for the pain, and I really didn't care what, just as long as it was a high dosage. I went through the formalities in the emergency room just as before. I explained to the nurse practitioner the pain in my legs and practically told her it was sciatica before she could speak. She said she'd noticed the way I walked and could tell my legs were in pain. She left the room for about ten minutes, and returned with a doctor who was briefed on my condition. They confirmed it was most likely sciatic nerve damage. I also told the medical doctor about the bursitis I was diagnosed with at the urgent care clinic. The doctor was very confused when I spoke about my prescribed antibiotics for bursitis. This was a bit concerning for me, but I was hopeful for any new information. It was settled that my sciatic nerves had caused the swelling, pain and discomfort in my legs. I was prescribed a twelve-day taper of steroids, essentially the reduction of a dose of a drug over a specified period of time. This taper of steroids would take the swelling down and alleviate the pain in my legs. With that, I was good to go, and I knew for certain I would get my life back in order.

PART TWO: HELLO AFRICA!

The flight to Cape Town, South Africa was very long, but the sheer excitement of traveling to the motherland far exceeded any angst about flying. With the dosage of steroids in my system, despite some leg cramps, it appeared most of my pain had gone away. I did, however, begin to experience a new side effect throughout the duration of the steroid taper: a constant itching all over my body. I was scratching my arms, legs and back like there was no tomorrow. Toy and I assumed it was from the steroids, and once the twelve-day taper was completed, the itching would stop.

As we made our way through customs, I observed the many shades of South Africans who resembled people I knew from the United States. The men had trimmed and tapered Afros and bald fades with razor sharp line-ups. I could tell Cape Town had some damn good barbers! I really felt alive, like I belonged. One of the workers took a second look at me, because he thought I was one of his co-workers—he mentioned this out loud. Usually, when people go on about me looking like another person, it becomes annoying.

This time I took it as a compliment, almost as a sign of endearment.

A driver waited for us once we retrieved our luggage. He was laid back and took his job of transporting volunteers very seriously. He explained that he would be our driver for the next several weeks, taking us to and from volunteer placements. I knew from my first impression of him that I would glean a great deal of knowledge and information from him in the weeks to come. I looked forward to learning not only about the people of Cape Town, but of Africa as a whole—and not just common information, but deep, soul-penetrating knowledge and facts others might elect to ignore. The driver had a calming spirit that made us feel very relaxed and welcomed.

The weather during the night of our arrival was in the low eighties, and the breeze was refreshing. I can recall the sense of stillness in the air. It was difficult to see the residential buildings and homes after we drove beyond an industrial area leading from the airport. I only saw tiny glimpses of the village homes and townships from the highway, and only because the driver pointed them out as we drove by. I found myself more intrigued by the apartment buildings, which I could see more clearly than the village homes. The apartment buildings resembled ones back in

America. As we continued on the highway, I noticed the tall fences and barbwires that surrounded many of the residential homes. We soon learned of the high crime rates in Cape Town, and how having a single security alarm was not enough. I also learned that socio-economic status played a major role in where the majority of homeowners lived. The effects of apartheid still lingered, although South Africa had been a democracy for almost twenty-years. The higher the poverty rate, no matter where you are in the world, the more likelihood of crime.

Before exiting the highway, we caught an amazing view of Downtown Cape Town. Lights were everywhere, similar to what you see in Chicago or New York City. There were tall buildings as well as shipping ports, and I thought about how active the nightlife would be, and how Toy and I could go out to enjoy the South African jazz scene, which was quite popular. My dream finally became my reality: I was in Africa. I became child-like. My initial experience in Africa was just like a kid in a candy store.

Our home for the next few weeks was a beautiful Victorian-style house. It was old and warm with tons of character, evident by the crackling sound echoing throughout the house when people walked about. I wouldn't get a full glimpse of its beauty until the next day, since it was late and most people were either asleep or out for the night. Toy was taken to her room, where she had a roommate, and I was taken to my room, located in the very back of the house. I stepped back, taking a full observation of my room. It wasn't a small room, nor was it large—somewhere in the middle. It made a lower-case *f* shape, if you can imagine. Unlike some of the other rooms in the house, it didn't have bunk beds, just two single beds. There were three windows—one small window over the sink, a large window across the room and a third window located horizontally to the bed I chose to sleep in. The windows were gated with enough space to ward off intruders, even birds. The windows had blinds, which for me was crucial, considering how much I enjoyed a bit of privacy.

There was a bathroom in the room as well, the kind of bathroom that has the sink, shower and toilet a foot away from each other. One of the volunteers told me that in Thailand, many of the bathrooms are constructed in this same manner. There was no carpeting, and I didn't have hardwood floors like in the other areas of the house—just dark-colored floor tiles. As I got ready for bed that night, I thought to myself how blessed I was to be in a new environment that would allow me to gain new perspectives. The driver told me breakfast was served at eight in the morning each day, and that I should probably rest up. His advice was well-intended, but I knew something he didn't. Rest for me wasn't coming easy, and although I was in a different setting and time zone, my pain and restlessness had traveled abroad with me.

Before I took a shower, I was still scratching my arms and now my upper chest like crazy. With the excitement of being in Africa, the scratching had become an afterthought, for a while. After the shower, I took a glance in the mirror and noticed small bruises forming on my upper chest where I had been scratching. My skin wasn't externally bleeding, so I assumed they were burn marks. The shower had poured out scalding hot water before I could get a proper temperature, so I thought the water must have burnt me a little. The shower did, however, provide temporary relief from the itching after the adjustment. Not very concerned with the bruises, I put on shorts and a t-shirt and got into bed, hoping to fall asleep soon enough.

***

The clock on my cellphone read 1:42 a.m., and I had closed my eyes at about 12:30 a.m. For a moment, I thought I had simply forgotten to adjust to the new time zone, but that wasn't the case. It was the same story as before: no sleep. I thought, since I had been traveling for over a day, I would be completely worn out and nothing in the world could stop me from passing out at the sight of a bed. Unfortunately, I found myself up in the middle of the night, listening to music and the wind whistling through the windows. This would continue for the next three nights. I learned the steroid taper had contributed to my sleepless nights. Now, instead of my eyes hurting from being open all the time, I was suddenly having bursts of energy. Not the kind of energy to run a marathon, but enough energy to be active.

As time passed, so did my hopes of getting sleep. As four in the morning rolled around, there I was, sitting on the edge of the bed with the night lamp on, trying to put the journal I'd brought with me to use. My first three nights were the only times I think I ever wrote in my journal. Whenever I look over those pages, I can see the anger in myself. Physically and mentally, I was unstable. Despite being granted the opportunity to be in Africa, I was angry that I was unable to enjoy those moments, as I had truly desired.

At five in the morning, I unpacked my luggage and placed my toiletries in the bathroom cabinets. This task didn't take long, so I shaved, took another shower and put my clothes on for the day. Around six in the morning, a South African bird started to make the most unique and craziest sound I had ever heard, reminding me that I was in a foreign country. It didn't sound like a pigeon or crow, but like a unique blow horn. The sound went *coo-coo-coo-koo-*

cuk-coo, and came in intervals of three. I'll admit the very first time I heard it, I really thought it was a dog with a bad throat. As the birds continued their chirping in the morning, I sat back on the bed fully dressed, ready to get the day started. I learned later that the bird was called a red-eyed dove.

At mealtime, the head chef rang a bell to let everyone know that food was ready to be served. At breakfast, I met more of the volunteers, some who had already been in Cape Town for weeks. I was the only male volunteer during my stay, but I had been raised by women for most of my life as a kid, so being around women for long periods of time was comforting.

All of the volunteers were enthusiastic and passionate about social service; it was great to be around like-minded individuals. We were all curious and open to learning more about one another. More importantly, we were all very excited to be volunteering our time to help those in need. For some of us, including myself, it was our first time. Others had volunteered abroad in other countries. Everyone shared their backgrounds, experiences and purpose for volunteering. Those who had volunteered in other countries spoke graciously of their previous experiences, while us first-timers were excited to create a new experience. I believe all of us knew we would get something very valuable in return from the people of South Africa. That value would be based on each individual and their personal perspective. I can only speak for myself when I say the value I received from the people of South Africa saved my life!

***

As a member of the most recent group of volunteers, the next two weeks had been planned for us. We started with a tour of downtown Cape Town and the surrounding areas of the city that were more developed in comparison to others. Before the tour started, we were informed that our tour scheduled for the following day, which included the townships and government housing area, would not be an easy sight to experience. I was very eager upon hearing this. I was curious as to what about the next day's tour would make me feel uncomfortable or uneasy.

From the highway, on our way to downtown, we could see beautiful mountains sitting like shoulder pads over the city. The two mountains we saw most often were Table Mountain and Lion's Head Mountain. Both were quite captivating. Their names fit perfectly—especially Lion's Head, which became my favorite. To me, the mountain represented strength and vitality, two things I seemed to be in search of. It truly resembled the top of a lion's head, when a lion lies on all four legs.

The first place we visited was the Castle of Good Hope;[2] it is the oldest standing building in Cape Town. The construction of the castle began in 1666, and upon its full completion, it served as a military quarters for the British and the Dutch. The castle served as a residence, a warehouse during the time of its operation—there were even shops, slave quarters and a church hall. It wasn't until 1917 that the Imperial government handed the Castle of Good Hope over to the South African government.

What struck me the most about the Castle were the five different country flags swaying at the walkway entrance. These were the flags of South Africa, the Dutch and Great Britain. We were told that the flags were placed in such order to represent the control over Cape Town from the start of slavery to the mid-1600s until 1917.[3] For me, it shows the

[2] The Castle of Good Hope is the oldest building in South Africa that is still in use. Art and photography exhibitions are often hosted within its five walls, as are some of the city's most premium commercial events. See http://www.capetown.travel/products/castle-of-good-hope http://www.news24.com/SouthAfrica/News/Shock-as-CTs-Castle-removes-old-SA-flag-20121123

[3] Since my initial visit to the Castle of Good Hope, the flags have been removed. See: http://www.defenceweb.co.za/index.php?option=com_content&view=article&id=28579:castle-told-to-remove-historical-flags&catid=111:sa-defence&Itemid=242. Also see

oppression of the South African people. It also represents the audacity of the British and Dutch to exchange rulership over a people by forcefully taking control of their land and resources. The enticing ports that extend off the coast of Cape Town was all it took for greed to overwhelm their minds and lead them to become heartless oppressors, thieves, and murderers.

***

My energy level was low during the tour, and I was really thankful when we drove long distances before the next destination. The driver took us to the top of Signal Hill Mountain, which displayed a glorious view of the coast of Cape Town and the Atlantic Ocean. We spent about fifteen to twenty minutes at the site and then walked back down a steep and curvy road to meet up with our driver. I remembered watching the other volunteers and Toy smiling and laughing as they took pictures, taking in the entire experience of Table Mountain. I took in about as much as I could. My body was still out of tune, and I found myself sitting down on rocks and benches more often. For a moment, when I looked at the ocean, I felt how fortunate I was to be in South Africa, viewing something only God could construct. The vastness of the ocean presented the endless possibilities of what life holds, and this was encouraging. At that moment, I felt as if anything was possible. Then I thought about Chicago, and growing up on the West Side.

Who knew that a black kid from the West Side of Chicago could travel abroad, touring one of the most beautiful places in the world with all odds against him. They counted me out, but I defeated the stereotype. I was not supposed to live without a purpose, my body does not belong behind prison bars, that life was not and is not for me, but that's what it's like being Black in America. According to The Sentencing Project[4], one in three black men will be imprisoned in their lifetime. Yet, as I looked out at the ocean, I realized — with physical pain or not, I was right where I was supposed to be. I didn't know why, exactly, but I had managed enough strength to make it this far. The view of the ocean gave me more hope. If I could make it to Africa, then millions of other Black young men and women could do it too. I decided from that point on, I would encourage all people to visit Africa especially people from the Black community.

---

[4] The Sentencing Project works for a fair and effective U.S. criminal justice system by promoting reforms in sentencing policy, addressing unjust racial disparities and practices, and advocating for alternatives to incarceration.

As we walked to meet our driver, we could see the beach homes and luxurious hotels along the coast. Cape Town is the perfect place to vacation, relax and enjoy the luxuries of life. I was there for another purpose, but I couldn't ignore the beautiful sceneries of the huge mountains surrounding the beachfront or the way the clouds floating above forming perfectly in the pure blue sky. Not even the most skilled photographer, with the top rated camera, could capture such majesty and one would have to be truly present in order to see the full scope of its magnificence.

As we got closer to the driver, we could see the South African Stadium, where the World Cup took place. Looking further to the left of the stadium, out on the ocean, was Robben Island, the place where the great Nelson Mandela spent most of his twenty-seven years of imprisonment. Despite the incomprehensible conditions, I was able to stand on the ground where he fought for an anti-apartheid South Africa and equal rights and opportunities for all, not only for Blacks, but for Whites as well. His desire for mankind to live in harmony together was truly extraordinary.

The next destination along our tour was the beachfront. Before arriving, we drove around and viewed the pristine homes and condominiums, like the ones seen on the Lifestyles of the Rich and Famous and MTV Cribs. I was delighted that we didn't have to walk for a while, so I could sit back with my shades on and possibly sleep for a bit. I recall being so tired, my energy continuing to diminish. By now, my arms were so sore from the steroid-induced scratching. Toy asked me several times if everything was okay, but she knew it wasn't, even when I told her differently. Her trust in me was more than I had in myself. I tried to convince myself that I could mask my discomfort since I was not the only person who had made the trip; there was no way I could let my issues affect her experience. I decided to keep my worsening pain to myself as much as possible.

Some people believe masks come only as physical objects, but there are those of us in life who know how and when to pull out an invisible mask. We can wear it well and even for a long time before it starts to fall apart. I personally had been wearing my invisible mask on and off for the past three years, and it wasn't until Toy and I began to get serious when I felt I could reveal myself more. I'd still kept my mask on in the past couple of months as I masked my physical, mental and, more importantly, spiritual pain with this invisible mask.

When we arrived at the beach, there were people all around having a great time. People were tanning and swimming, kids splashing water on each other and happiness was all around. While some of the other volunteers walked closer to the beach, I knew I wouldn't be able to get that far without more energy. I decided to stay near the tour bus and sat on some huge rocks off the shore. I sat alone for a moment as I watched the waves crash into the shore. The sounds of the waves gliding along and rushing into the rocks provided me with a comforting sound. The harmony gave me a sense of peace after the water retreated back into the ocean. It was a familiar calmness that I felt. It felt similar to the night I had stood out on the edge of the docks on Lake Michigan on Lake Shore Drive.

***

I can recall a night in February 2008, in Chicago. The wind chill was mighty as ever, and snow piled high everywhere. I pulled over on Lake Shore Drive at Thirty-First Street and drove into the parking lot. I got out of my car, avoiding looking at myself in either the rearview mirror or side mirrors. I didn't want to see my face, the ugly truth: I wanted to take my own life. At the time, I was conceiving thoughts of suicide. A slight cut to the wrist, perhaps, but this idea left open the possibility of survival—even despite this realization, I still intended to end my life. The troubles I thought I had at the time were many, and I didn't want to face them anymore.

I would commute to work by train from time to time, and the idea of jumping in front of a train was a thought I pondered as well. Even driving fast and hard into a light pole was an option. The light pole idea was nearly acted out, and it was certainly close enough. After I swerved back onto the road, I looked in the rearview mirror and cursed at myself, focusing completely on driving home. However, standing on a dock on Lake Michigan, it became apparent that nothing had changed as I stared down at the pieces of frozen water. Here was my final destination; no one else was out there but me. It was unlike the crowded train stations, and I wouldn't be pulled from the car at a light pole. There would be no sliding a knife across my wrist. The most I would have to do would be to jump.

I thought about what it would feel like after I jumped into the water. I thought of the freezing cold water that would engulf my brain and body. I imagined it to be slow and agonizing, and I would be in excruciating pain, unable to come up for air. Suddenly, I felt the wind blowing hard enough to make me stumble back. A couple of huge waves hit the rocks and docks with great force, and I took more steps back as the water retreated back into the lake. A sense of calm came over me, and I was at peace for a moment. I could hear a voice inside me say, "Everything will be okay; turn around and go home." As I walked backed to my car, at a much faster pace, I wondered whose voice spoke to me that night. I hoped it was my grandmother, Dorothy, who had died in 2002, because I often believed she had become my guardian angel.

As I drove home, still wondering about the voice I had heard, I thought maybe it was her. I didn't come up with an answer that night, but I now know that voice that spoke inside me that night was the same one that had spoken to me many times before.

Since the night on Lake Michigan, the idea of taking my own life completely went away. The irony, of course, is that my troubles and trials were still present. I understood more clearly that this is all a part of life's journey. Trials and troubles come to everyone; I understood after my incident on Lake Michigan that mine weren't single-handedly picking me out of the billions of people in the world. That's not how it works; on Lake Michigan, I finally got a sense of that and began to get back on track. My intent was pure, maybe noble, but I was still naïvely in my own way. Still, I felt my soul encouraging me to pull up my bootstraps and do whatever I needed to do to live better. The art of dealing with life's tribulations is through perseverance. No matter what, you can never give up. I was beginning to learn this valuable life lesson.

Disclaimer:

It is not my intent nor do I encourage one to commit suicide or bring harm to their bodies. I am only expressing my feelings and emotions through the artistic form of writing by describing a space I once found myself in years ago. However, it is my hope, to encourage anyone who may have feelings of loneliness, inadequacy and/or trouble overcoming a life trauma, to seek professional or spiritual guidance to find a reason to live. If you find yourself in a situation to where you feel like harming yourself and feel that suicide is your only solution, please DO NOT HESITATE to call the National Suicide Prevention Lifeline. By calling 1-800-273-TALK (8255) you'll be connected to a skilled, trained counselor at a crisis center in your area, anytime 24/7.

SUICIDE PREVENTION RESOURCE:

National Suicide Prevention Lifeline

Website: https://suicidepreventionlifeline.org

Telephone: 1-800-273-TALK (8255)

Lifeline (@800273TALK) | Twitter

***

Some of the sights at the beachfront reminded me of South Beach Florida, where restaurants are built side-by-side and people dine on patios that extend to the sidewalks. I also noticed luxurious homes, condominiums and fancy cars, but what garnered my attention most was the lack of black people residing in these particular areas. For me, it was a clear sign that Cape Town, like many major cities in the U.S., had a distribution problem. The wealth distribution gap between black South Africans and white South Africans was greatly disproportionate, though some improvements had been made since the country created a democracy after the apartheid. I was reminded that in the U.S., the wealth gap between socioeconomic classes continues to grow. For example, a Washington Post analysis of data from the Federal Reserve Survey of Consumer Finances states on average white families hold seven times the wealth of black families. The efforts of the programs and policies in place to assure people of non-privilege get afforded the same opportunities as those in more fortunate situations is noble and admirable, but at that moment, progress to me seemed nonexistent.

Though the first part of our tour was enlightening and wonderful, by the time we returned to our home-base I was completely worn out and it wasn't even five o'clock. I wanted to get to my room and go to sleep, but was still very excited and curious about the upcoming tours of the townships and black communities. So it came as no surprise that during my second night I laid in bed wide-awake, thoughts of sheer excitement rushing through my body. My attempt at writing in my journal failed immensely, and was met only with restlessness, pain and frustration. All I could do was hope that there were better days to come, and focus on volunteering to fill my mind.

I finally dozed off for a couple of hours. I guess I couldn't complain too much, given that the previous night I hadn't slept at all. At 7:00 a.m., I got ready for the day and met more of the volunteers during breakfast. We had all come from completely different paths and careers, but we shared one common goal: to be of service to others the best way we could. For me, it didn't matter what any of our differences might be, whether political, religious or our childhood upbringings, as well as previous perceptions we may have developed of people outside our immediate community. I admired these people because they cared. They cared enough to travel thousands of miles to help those in need, who could offer a different perspective on life. I can safely assume that some of the volunteers encountered opposition as to why it was necessary to travel abroad to help others when many people in America need help as well.

True, many Americans do suffer the same fate as those we came to serve in Africa, but this experience was different. After carefully considering their concern of my urgency to volunteer abroad, my response was simply, "perspective." I wanted to gain perspective. When I decided to volunteer abroad, I did so with the desire of gaining new perspectives about the world as a whole, so I turned "Why?" into "Why not?" The necessity of gaining new and different perspectives was crucial to my growth and walk in life. I realized more than ever how similar we are as a people and also how fortunate some of us are to have certain necessities like clean water, food or simply better resources to take care of ourselves and our families. It was absolutely essential I recognize and embrace this aspect of life.

We had a tour guide with us as we went to the townships and black communities of Cape Town. Our tour guide was a South African native, who was very knowledgeable and insightful. The first place we visited was called District 6[5], a product of apartheid. When we pulled up, I saw nothing but an empty vast space on a grassy hill. Beyond this area were fences at the top of the hill, surrounded by apartment flats and houses. On the west side of the area was an elementary school. As we were viewing District 6, we had the privilege of seeing several classes of students heading out for recess. They were dressed in green

---

[5] District Six was named the Sixth Municipal District of Cape Town in 1867. Originally established as a mixed community of freed slaves, merchants, artisans, laborers and immigrants, see http://www.districtsix.co.za

and yellow uniforms and became very excited when they saw us from a distance. They smiled and shouted, "Hello!" and we replied with just as much excitement. Our tour guide explained to us that District 6, at one point, housed more than sixty thousand residents of mixed descent. During the 1970s, the apartheid government of South Africa declared the area to be whites-only and forced out the other races.

The first groups of descendants to be forced out of District 6 were black South Africans, who, despite their protests, were placed in the townships and flats of Cape Town's isolated plains. We learned that after all the residents had been forced out, their homes were torn down. The community and culture developed by the people who had lived in District 6 was destroyed as well. The area is still empty to this day, because of on-going protests and developers refusing to build anything in the area. As our tour guide gathered us together to head to the next site, I realized I was getting my first real look at the monster known as apartheid, created in South Africa. As we headed to the next site, the fatigue I felt appeared to be a new aspect in my life. My legs weighed me down as I fought for strength to push along on the tour. My curiosity was my only motivation to keep moving forward. I wanted to learn more about the black people living in the townships and communities.

The next place we visited was the Trojan Horse Memorial, located in the Athlone area of Cape Town. The Memorial commemorates three anti-apartheid teenagers who were killed and fifteen others wounded during a police ambush of the area in 1985. The police hid in the back of a truck and as it rode through the neighborhood, and the people threw pebbles and rocks as the truck rode by. As the villagers carried out this act of protest, the police revealed themselves from the back of the truck and opened gunfire. The horrifying events of District 6 and the Trojan Horse Massacre only fueled my anger toward those who employ greed and envy as a means of performing inhumane activities.

While driving to the next site, I noticed a quietness settle among the group. Unlike the ride from the previous day, today was not as cheerful—to say the least. For me, it was one thing to hear about people being forcefully removed from their homes and communities, but to hear and learn about innocent teenagers and children being murdered took things to a whole new level. The concept of murder puts the mind into deep contemplation.

We drove into a black South African community of apartment flats. From the van, we could see people hanging outside and socializing. It was a Monday, and most of the kids were in school. There were a lot of preschoolers playing around along with high school boys and girls. As we got out of the van in what appeared to be the central area of the flats, we saw three vendors selling South African jewelry, clothes, paintings and other merchandise, along with famous vuvuzela horns. We were clearly at a highly populated tourist attraction. Another van that actually had a tour guide and labels on its sides confirmed this. We were volunteers, not tourists, at least in my mind. I tried to find a happy medium between the two as I saw hundreds of people flood the area.

From there, our tour guide took us inside one of the apartments, and we saw two table benches about two feet wide and eight feet long that extended from the walls. There was one table on the right side, and one table on the left side of the room. On the right, in the corner, was a small kitchen sink. There were no cabinets, dishwasher or stove. There was one bathroom on each side, no bigger than an airplane restroom; paint chipped off the walls, and dilapidated floor tiles were chipping away as well. Our tour guide explained how the flats were originally built to house migrant workers who traveled far away from their families and homelands. When the jobs were gone, the flats remained. These small apartment flats were residences to four different families, housing sixteen or more people at a time. On average, families of four shared one room with a kitchen sink, toilet and one shower on each side of the apartment.

There was a time in my childhood when twenty of my family members—brothers, sisters, cousins, aunts, uncles and grandmothers—lived under one roof. It was an apartment as well, but unlike the flats, we had a living room, dining room, two bedrooms, one bathroom and a kitchen with a stove, sink, table and chairs. We did, however, turn every room into sleeping areas, and still had some space to move amongst each other. But as I stood inside the apartment flats, I couldn't wrap my mind around the idea of living in such a condensed space.

After we left the apartment, we went to purchase merchandise: t-shirts, necklaces, keychains and bags from the vendors. The sun was scorching and I really wanted to get back into the tour van. Before I did, I noticed another vendor about twenty feet away from the other two. He didn't have multiple tables of merchandise—only a board standing about three feet tall filled with earrings. These earrings were beautiful and made out of all sorts of materials like copper wires that were designed in hoops and swirls with feathers attached. The seller appeared to be very young, perhaps fourteen or sixteen years old. I assumed he was trying to make money to help support his family, rather than being in school like most boys his age. I was learning that adult responsibilities as a black South African came at a very early age.

***

Young children always bring smiles to people's faces, even when they aren't aware of it!

After leaving the apartment flats, we visited a place with a daycare, a professional development center and outreach center for black South African women living with HIV/AIDS. I remember feeling so fatigued on the way to the center, but once we arrived and were informed about the services, I became more alert, especially with the mention of HIV/AIDS. During this time, I still harbored complete disdain in my heart for this incurable disease, and it only deepened when we met women who were directly affected by it. They were knitting and sewing, making colorful blankets, bracelets and necklaces and other things. When I saw the women were all black, the bitterness added more fire to my rage. I thought about the time they had until their death and wondered if they were as angry as I was about the absence of a cure.

As we headed to the daycare, my thoughts went to the children of the mothers who had been affected with HIV/AIDS. What about the children born into this disease? These thoughts consumed my mind as we traveled to our next location. My mind was captivated from a worldly perspective, but this was one place highly populated with the disease—what about the rest of the world? This not only affects the community, but several families and countries as a global epidemic. My mind and heart were on two different pages in the same book. Everyone deserves the opportunity to live a prosperous and fulfilling life.

The construction of the daycare was very nice. It had a second floor for the children to take naps. There was a classroom for the older children, who sang songs for us and taught us their unique names. The children were like sponges as they tried to mimic our language and the high-fives we gave. They were so excited and free, living life to the fullest, which is how it should be. I've learned recently that inspiration and encouragement can come in the form of a friend or a stranger; someone can re-ignite the fire of a dream.

I realized this during my stay at the hospital back home. I was on the phone with my best friend. "I believe God works through people and delivers his message through people," he said. "D, most events in life aren't a coincidence!"

As the children played on the center's playground, I took a deep breath and sat on the wooden steps near the door. My legs were beginning to hurt, and the itching started to become unbearable. As I became worn down from the lack of energy, I noticed a young boy who was practically manhandling a car tire. "Don't ever stop pushing forward, little man," is what I wish I could have said to him. Who knows if he would have understood me. One can only dream, right?

Before ending the tour, we made one more stop to another daycare. This daycare was smaller than the previous one. Although we were in a different place, the joyful spirit of the children remained the same, and they were just as excited to see us and sing songs like the others. We arrived at a time when some of the children were taking naps. I remember seeing a little boy sitting on the floor with one of those old school cellphones that look like a large brick. He was sitting still the entire time, watching all the activities take place, except when the time came for us to leave. Then I noticed he was doing what I craved the most: sleep.

We had been touring the township of Langa for the latter part of the tour, and the time for us to get back for lunch was drawing near. This meant we couldn't visit the second township on the schedule, Khayelitsha. This was a bit of a disappointment, because it was the township I had been assigned to for my volunteer placement. I thought it would be great to see the area before my first day. Still, I remained optimistic about the new opportunity. The guide informed us that Khayelitsha is the largest and fastest growing township in Cape Town. Although I was nervous for being the only volunteer placed in the Khayelitsha Township, I was excited, yet curious.

***

I was assigned to volunteer at the Khayelitsha site in Cape Town, South Africa, during the week of March 28. When I arrived, I remember thinking the school looked similar to the one from the movie *Sarafina!* I was led into the school's office building, and met briefly with the principal. A teacher, who favored my grandmother, escorted me to a classroom. The resemblance came from her short grayish hair that was slightly curly. Her hair was a bit longer, and she had mocha-colored skin, but she was probably the same age as my grandmother. One thing was sure: like my grandmother, this teacher was loving and kind.

When we walked into the classroom, the students were seated in three rows on long bench tables. There were forty or more students in the classroom. They looked at me with great curiosity. I knew I was supposed to be there, but they had no clue who I was. I was led to the back of the classroom to the teacher's desk. The language barrier between me and my escort began to occur by this time. She tried to explain the lesson plan to me, but I just couldn't understand. We eventually found a balance, where she began to point out certain subjects in the books and I nodded my head "yes" or "no," to show her I understood.

In Khaylelitsha, the native language is Xhosa, and to my luck I only spoke English. In other areas of Cape Town, they use the Afrikaans or English language. But the students I was working with, and mostly all the teachers and staff, communicated in Xhosa with very limited English. My escort informed me that the school would need me to step in as a teacher instead of what I was expecting to be, a teacher's aide. The actual teacher of the class had personal matters to attend to and the school was short on staff. Not only did I need to be acting as the teacher for the day, but for the rest of the week. My initial reaction was excitement, because I had strongly considered becoming a teacher in the States. So of course, I was ecstatic at the opportunity.

The students were sixth graders, and I was instructed to teach them how to write in English and to share my experiences of living in the U.S.A. *No problem*, I thought. *I love young people, especially in this age group.* I had definitely enjoyed any opportunities to speak in front of young people about life experiences. I always tried to give encouraging and positive outlooks on life, especially in regard to education and staying in school. I was once told that knowledge is only potential power, because even though you can retain a lot of knowledge, it still has to be applied to be effective. Unfortunately for me at this time, I was obtaining a lot of knowledge, but lacked the courage to effectively put that knowledge into action.

My escort introduced me to the class in Xhosa, and from my understanding I believe she told the students to be on their best behavior and follow my instructions. When she left the classroom, there was a long moment of silence. The nervous tension we all shared couldn't have been more obvious. One of the first questions I asked after writing my name on the chalkboard was if they had any questions for me. I received more silence in return, along with gleaming faces staring right back at me, eager to learn or do something. Before I had arrived in the classroom, they had been working on an assignment. After I cluelessly walked around the classroom, I could hear soft chuckles fill the room. I stepped outside for a second. It wasn't that it was hot or warm in the classroom—I was still so nervous, and couldn't find the right way to connect with the students.

I looked to the sky. "Please, God, give me some guidance on this situation," I asked.

I took a deep breath and went back inside the classroom. When I walked back in, the students began watching my every movement. I was like a deer in headlights. Where was I to go from here? I immediately asked them to go around the room and state their names. As they went around stating their names, one by one, I tried my best to repeat them, until after the tenth student or so I began to notice I was just mumbling words back to them in a lower voice. Their names were so beautiful. Each of them, I'm sure, had a meaning behind it. After the quick name activity, I was back where I was before. Silence. The name sharing activity hadn't taken as long as I had hoped.

Once again, I found myself walking back outside, right after I instructed them to complete the same assignment they had already completed. Again, I looked up to the sky and took a deep a breath. There wasn't a need to speak words; I just needed more assurance I was where I was supposed to be. When I stepped back into the classroom this

time, I began to get a feeling I would never forget; it stayed
with me for the rest of week during my time with the
students. I picked up a piece of chalk and wrote the word
DREAMS on the chalkboard. I'm not sure what made me take
this route, but I am a believer in following your dreams. It
doesn't matter to me if you are a five-year-old child or a
middle-aged high level corporate executive. It doesn't matter
the age—if you tell me about a dream or something you've
always wanted to do, I encourage you to go out and do it.
Perhaps I went this route because I still believed in my very
own dreams, and subconsciously had still been chasing them.

I personally thought I wasn't chasing my dreams due
to my lack of courage. For years, I had talked about visiting
Africa—specifically Nigeria, where my father's roots
originated. My paternal grandfather had died in Nigeria
when I was two years old. He was born and raised in Lagos,
Nigeria. My African American grandmother tried to imitate
his voice and speak with his accent to describe his sentiments
about his native country. As my curiosity grew to know more
about grandfather, I became more interested in visiting
Africa. I still feel pride in knowing that I can directly trace
my roots to Africa, even with limited information about my
grandfather. Unlike many other African Americans, I have
been afforded this privilege to know my ancestry. As I

learned more about the importance of identity in my family name, I felt more connected to Africa.

I asked the students to tell me about their dreams.

"What do dreams mean to you?" I asked.

I didn't get any responses, just blank stares.

Thankfully, I didn't lose their attention, because despite the language barrier, they were still able to understand me. I didn't give up on my dream concept just yet. At this age, I believe kids dream and explore with their imaginations from time to time without being discouraged to do so. This presented an opportunity for me to let these kids know that anything is possible. Maybe, just maybe, a seed or two could be planted in their minds about the unlimited possibilities, regardless of the circumstances they grew up in or what hand they'd been dealt in life. I asked my students to go around the classroom and tell me what they wanted to do in life.

The career goals of the sixth graders were quite surprising. In addition to teachers, they wanted to be social workers, police officers, civil engineers, presidents, entrepreneurs—and I even got a fashion designer. As I wrote these careers on the chalkboard, it dawned on me that none of them mentioned playing a professional sport or being a celebrity entertainer. I find nothing wrong with professional athletes and entertainers of the world; however, these careers seemed to be a lot less enticing to these sixth graders than those I've spoken with back home.

Thinking back to when I was in the sixth grade, all I thought about being was a professional basketball player, because it was cool; it could bring my family and me lots of money and a chance to get out of the ghetto. A career of being a teacher or a police officer had not been high on my aspirational list. Author Mark Twain once said, "Whenever you find yourself on the side of the majority, it's time to pause and reflect." Well, at that age, I wasn't pausing or reflecting. I just wanted to play basketball and own a pair of ` Jordan sneakers. These sixth graders were different; they were far more evolved than I had been at their age. Most importantly, they were more aware and willing to give back and become contributing citizens in their communities. Glamour and fame didn't appeal to them, and I was impressed.

In order to stay within the lesson plan, I asked the students to explain in writing why they were interested in their chosen careers. I quickly learned that not all of the students would initially be motivated to do classroom work. These students needed a little more push and encouragement. I respect teachers who commit to this difficult task every day in order to educate future leaders. The responsibility and impact of a teacher can leave a lasting impression on a young mind. As I graded their assignments, it was clear these students were aware of their surroundings even more than I had thought. Collectively, those who completed the assignment on my initial request wrote about improving their communities, schools and city. It was a true honor to have them share their stories. Their courage to push beyond their current circumstances was remarkable, to say the least.

When the bell rang for lunch, all of the students looked at me and waited for permission to leave. Once I realized what they were doing I was very impressed and smiled. Permission granted, they took off and headed outside to play with the other students. My day with them ended at this time. While I waited for transportation, some of the students came to ask me questions about America, the land of opportunity.

***

During my stay at the school, a couple of students would try diligently to teach me the Xhosa language. I tried and they tried with great excitement, until I finally got one word correct: "Sebonana." It means, "See you later!"

"Sebonana" was my departing word to them for the remainder of the week.

Not long after, I learned from Dr. Cornel West that, specifically in regard to young people, all it takes is to plant one seed of encouragement. Dr. West says, "You only have to plant the seed in the mind and not try to stay to cultivate its growth." One of the main objectives in influencing youth is to get to as many as possible. You should try to plant the seed and keep moving on to the next one, he advises. When I first heard this, I had already left South Africa and was in a hospital room back in the States, but it made me think about my time in the classroom with the students.

One of the most eye-opening moments I had in South Africa happened on my second day in the classroom. I heard some of the students mumbling to each other, and I asked what was going on. Then, after a bit of encouragement from some classmates, one of the students stood and handed me some papers. On these papers, she had drawn and colored several dresses and blouses, because on the previous day, she had shared her dream of being a fashion designer. I had simply told her that she didn't have to wait to be an adult to start her dream; she could start right then. It took me by surprise, and I couldn't find the words to actually respond when I saw what she had gone home to create. I let her know that the dresses and blouses were gorgeous, writing "Excellent" at the top of the pages. I gave the papers back to her and let her know she should keep them for herself. I only hoped that they could serve as a reminder for her to chase after her dream(s).

Often I think about this moment. Before learning about the lesson of planting seeds from Dr. West, I had wondered how this student would be motivated to be a fashion designer without someone giving her more encouragement. However, I realized that all it took was for her to be told that she could be a fashion designer. As the old adage goes, "If it ain't written, it don't exist!" This served as enough validation for me that she will be just fine to go after her dream; her actions to live out her dream on a basic piece of paper took a lot of courage.

I expect to see her dresses and blouses on models someday. There's nothing wrong with a little hope, right?

***

The food at our home-base was always good. I found myself eating foods I normally wouldn't have eaten, which was one of the benefits of traveling abroad. Lunch was a good time for me, not only because of the food, but also because of the stories. All the volunteers and staff would eat together and share stories about their day. It never failed to amaze me, hearing about the children at the schools and daycares, or the courageous women at the shelters and the centers, doing whatever necessary to live and enjoy life. It was also a joy to hear about the staff's personal life stories.

It became routine after lunch to head to my room, take my steroids, kick my shoes off and jump into bed. This may have been the only time where my body shut down long enough to actually rest. I was so grateful for Toy, who continued to be by my side throughout this very rough time of my life. She would check up on me after lunch and bring so much positive energy. At night when I struggled to sleep, Toy would stay up with me for as long as she could, encouraging me that everything would be okay and to let go of my worries. She assured me that the pain would soon pass. During these sleepless nights, she would remind me we had made it to Africa and that we were helping people, while also gaining so much for ourselves. I am and will continue to be grateful and thankful for her presence in my life; I know it's no coincidence that our lives crossed paths. In many of my darkest times, it was her light that gave me hope to believe things would be better.

PART THREE: You Only Need an Ounce of Faith *(Mustard Seed of Faith)*

At the end of our first weekend, we had lunch at ROCA Restaurant on the Dieu Donne Vineyards in Franschhoek, South Africa. We could see a magnificent view of the Franschhoek Mountains from the outdoor patio where we dined. We ordered a variety of meals ranging from seafood to beef entrees. I ordered a bowl of mussels with garlic bread. Toy was a bit bolder with her meal selection. She ordered Zebra, and simply stated, "It's gamey!" when asked about her meal.

After lunch, we went to Stellenbosch for a wine tour. At one of the vineyards we stayed for about an hour. One of the hosts escorted us to picnic tables behind the wine distillery barn. We were given different tastings of wine and the host told us about the history of the vineyard and about the day-to-day operations. Everyone in the group was so elated. We all seemed to be in a space of great peace as we shared our thoughts and feelings about our experiences in Cape Town thus far.

The following week, for me, would be spent volunteering at Blikkiesdorp, a temporary relocation area for South Africans. Blikkiesdorp is in Delft, Cape Town. The shacks in Blikkiedorp were not very large—and roughly measured to be ten by twenty feet in size. They were constructed to house four different families to share one outdoor water faucet and a toilet. The number of family members in each shack ranged from six to eight people. The shacks were built on sand and dust-filled grounds. Upon entry into the site, there was a vast open space. On windy days the sand and dust flew everywhere.

It was a holiday or vacation week for most of the school-aged children. At this placement, I was paired with another volunteer. We assisted a group of people from an awareness organization. The awareness organization was there to help children focus on adopting proper hygiene habits and provide them with safety procedures in case of an emergency, or unfortunately in some cases how to report physical and sexual abuse. When we arrived on the first day, an older gentleman greeted us. He appeared to be in his late fifties to sixties, and volunteered to assist families in the living area on what resources were available to them. He was very genuine and nice to us, and even took time to tell us about the creation of the temporary area and the structure of the shacks. Inside the office, which was a storage trailer, he played gospel music from a radio. This genre of music would not change throughout the rest of the week that we were there.

He explained that the housing authority of the Cape Town government basically dumped homeless people and those on the waiting list for government housing in the Blikkiesdorp area. He said he had been on the waiting list for more than eighteen years. We also met another man, with a disabled leg, who had been on the waiting list for twenty-three years. The man with the disabled leg could not understand that a person eighteen years old could receive a home sooner than he did. What was even more disturbing to him was that the eighteen-year-old was said to be on the waiting list for over twenty years. It didn't add up to this man—or to me, for that matter. Both the older man and the man with a disabled leg both agreed that Blikkiesdorp had the worst living conditions in all of the townships built during the apartheid.

The awareness programs started off with fifty kids, and then increased to seventy-five and then to more than a hundred by the end of the week. The kids aged from two years old to twelve years old, and I saw six-year-olds watching over their two-year-old siblings. Responsibility for these young children started early in life, and a lot of the kids were not wearing shoes or sandals, despite the conditions of sand and dust on the ground and rocks scattered everywhere. The awareness program focused on issues these kids experienced on a daily basis. The educational activities included alcohol abuse, child abuse, proper hygiene methods and ways to contact police and fire officials in case of an emergency.

The kids were really enthusiastic about the activities. More so, the kids were able to get a meal at the end of each day once the activities were done. For most of the kids, this would be their only meal for the day. Throughout the week, my awareness of poverty had increased. In all honesty, I had never witnessed such poor conditions as I witnessed in certain areas of Cape Town. Even my own humble beginnings seemed like a four-star hotel experience in comparison.

What was undeniable was the youthful exuberance displayed by the kids in Blikkiesdorp and those kids in the Langa and Khayelitsha townships. With very limited resources, these kids still enjoyed life by playing cricket, hand-clapping games and soccer. Regardless of their social and economic conditions, they lived in the moment. Unfortunately, if the problems surrounding them didn't improve along with major changes, these kids would continue to be set up for failure, and injustice would continue to prevail.

* * *

One sure thing I noticed about the South African people living in this temporary area and those in other townships was the unshakeable and unwavering amount of faith. Faith ran deep among the South African people. The more I conversed with South Africans whether they were "Black," "Colored," "Indian" or "White," the more I witnessed it. They showed a belief in a better tomorrow and had an immeasurable gratitude for living in the present moment.

What I witnessed from the people of South Africa was hope. A hope that the future would bring more justice and prosperity to people who have been deprived of such things for more than four hundred years, as well as those who constantly fight for more justice regardless of their skin color or gender. The faith, displayed by the gentleman with the disabled leg in Blikkiesdorp was astonishing. He believed, without a shadow of a doubt, that he and his family would get a house, despite being on the waiting list for more than twenty-three years. This was inspiration for me.

I couldn't understand how people could remain so hopeful, despite their severe circumstances. Perhaps I had possessed that same faith at one time, early in my life, but I had given up on it when I had chosen not to be in agreement with God. My paternal grandmother possesses similar characteristics of faith as the people in South Africa; it's the unyielding belief that things will get better. Another important person in my life who possesses this belief is Toy. No matter what is going on and how low the chips may fall, these two women maintain a sense of faith for better days to come.

I was finally observing faith in a way I had never experienced. I couldn't place my finger on what drove these people to have such deep convictions. Yet as I interacted, communicated and observed the South African people, especially in Blikkiesdorp, I saw the peace and gratitude they had to simply be alive, while living daily in hope. One thing I knew for certain by my third day in Blikkiesdorp was that if I could get an ounce of their faith, just a mustard seed's worth, I would be just fine for the remainder of my life's journey.

***

It's funny how life works out, or maybe it's funny how God listens to us when we least expect it. I had completed my steroid taper the week I volunteered in Blikkiesdorp, and with time I began to feel a little better. Thankfully, my legs weren't in pain, and my fatigue level had gone down. On Wednesday, I felt as if my condition was improving.

On Thursday, I begin to feel a little uneasy as we played role-playing games about safety procedures with the children at the awareness program. I began to have massive headaches and found myself sitting down as often as I could. I took some Ibuprofen, which relieved some of the pain, but by Friday morning I was working on two hours of sleep and my fatigue felt stronger than ever. By the time I made it to the placement for the final day, the pain became unbearable as my head throbbed and my eyes hurt to even stay open.

Soon enough, someone from the awareness group took notice of my condition; I was sweating profusely and my body was painfully weak. One of the women from the awareness program asked if I was okay and I responded in pain with the request of much-needed sleep. I was unaware of what was happening to me, but I could tell no one else knew either.

***

That Friday evening, Toy and I made plans for dinner at Mama Africa in downtown. My energy was low, but I was determined to remain strong. I remember being unbelievably tired as I tried to choose an outfit to wear for the evening. I was barely hungry, and the medicine showed no promise of relieving the pain any time soon.

When Saturday arrived, I wanted to take a few multivitamins to supplement my energy loss, especially since I had tapered off steroids for a few days. While others went out and enjoyed their Saturday embracing the beauty of Cape Town, I found it easier to stay at the home. I should have paid more attention to my health. But I decided to head to the mall and buy vitamin supplements. Even that day, it took me twenty minutes to take a shower, because I was having trouble catching my breath from the hot air. Everything became more clear as each event happened. It took more than ten minutes to put on socks, pants and a shirt, when it typically took me two seconds. The daunting task of putting on a pair of socks that day was as draining as running a marathon.

Still, despite these signs, I was determined to see myself in a better condition. There was nothing that was going to hold me down long enough to keep me still. Finally, after getting dressed, I called for a taxi and headed to the mall. When I arrived, I became aware that I couldn't walk for more than a minute or two without stopping to catch my breath. I finally made it to a shop selling vitamins, and I bought a pack. The clerk behind the counter assured me the vitamins would be effective. I also purchased a bottle of water for my presumed dehydration. I wasn't confident about the chewable vitamin C tablets, so I decided to keep looking for alternative options.

Again, with every passing minute I would have to stop, catch my breath and try to exert more energy. To no surprise, the mall was crowded with people, and at times I couldn't find a bench to sit on. In fact, during one of my stops, I actually sat on the floor near a wall. I knew it was time for me to get back to the base. I called a taxi and made my way back. I remember somewhat stumbling back into my room, and uncontrollably falling into bed. It was such a relief to be lying down; and that's where I remained for the rest of the day and night.

"Just give me the strength," is all I kept repeating to myself, as I laid in bed. When Toy came to see me, I could tell by her concerned expression that I didn't look too well. I explained my episode at the mall, and she wasn't too pleased that I'd gone out on my own. I tried to explain to her that I'd wanted to push myself in hopes of getting better. Unfortunately, the vitamins didn't do much at all. Not that I'd truly expected them to, but I was hopeful.

The next day, Toy and I decided to go out for brunch, and again it took me more than thirty minutes to get ready. It must have been ninety-five degrees that day, because I was sweating into the leather seats in the taxi as we headed to the restaurant. Luckily the taxi driver turned on the air conditioning, so I was able to cool off as we listened to music on the radio that reminded me of home.

When we arrived at the restaurant, both Toy and I ordered blueberry French toast with bacon. The food looked amazing, but my loss of appetite prevented me from devouring the plate in front of me. My energy was too low to eat much of anything. The restaurant was fairly empty during this time. It might have just been a down time period in general, but I only recall interacting with Toy and our waiter. We sat in an open area at a table for two. From my seat I could see outdoors and the sunlight seemed to get brighter by the minute. Toy took notice of how I hardly touched my food and asked if the food was okay, but by this time she had grown accustomed to my up and down appetite—or the lack thereof. I told her it wasn't the food, because the small amount I did ingest was delicious. My entire body felt weak and I continue to sweat. Every few seconds I was patting my forehead with one of the table napkins. I continued to gulp down water, glass after glass, but my body still remained weary.

As we left the restaurant and slowly walked towards the taxi, I suddenly lost all strength to walk on my own. I had to lean on Toy's shoulder for support, just to make it safely back to the taxi. Later that night, and many times after, I wondered what would have happened to me if Toy wasn't there. My imagination started to unfold. What happened if I passed out? Being stranded in the middle of Cape Town was definitely a possibility with the onset symptoms. Although these thoughts entered my mind, I was grateful that this was not the case. However, it allows me now to realize the blessing in front of me, which further lets me know that each of us are not meant to walk this journey of life alone!

**

Immediately after I went to bed, Toy took control. The next day, she said, I was going to see a doctor and she would make the appointment. As I tried to fall asleep that night, I found my mind and body to be restless, tossing and turning throughout the sheets. I wondered more and more of what could be going on. I went through scenario after scenario. Maybe I was experiencing the flu again, or even experiencing kidney failure I thought for some reason. I thought of all sorts of ailments to put a name on what I was experiencing physically. My mental state was gone, as my focus to detail diminished more with each passing day.

When it was time to leave for the doctor's office the following morning, I was in terrible shape. I remember walking through brown double doors as I entered into the clinic. A receptionist, who directed us to the waiting area where other people were seating, greeted us. The waiting area was a simple hallway with a few plastic red chairs on each side of the wall, and the floors were white tile. As we entered the doctor's office, which was a big room with a desk, chairs and exam table, she immediately noticed the pale discoloration of my skin. She even considered me depressed. I was approaching my breaking point and offered no rebuke when she made her observation. The doctor arranged for me to have lab work done immediately after she checked my vitals. I was evaluated for anemia and potential thyroid issues. As I sat in the doctor's room, getting my blood taken, I knew for certain I was suffering from one or the other. In my previous visits to the hospitals back home, I had never been checked for either of the two. This was both relieving and nerve-wracking, because I was unsure why these particular observations were so obvious to the doctor in South Africa and not the doctors I'd seen in the States. Even when I thought back to my own self-diagnosis, it was disconcerting that the doctors back home had opted not to run more tests to be certain.

Around nine o'clock that evening, I received a call from the doctor who had examined me and ordered the lab work. I was told I was severely anemic and required medical attention first thing the next morning. The doctor made arrangements for me to see the head doctor of hematology at a private hospital in Cape Town. I was extremely grateful for the time she spent after hours following up, along with the results of my illness. Toy and I were elated with the doctor's phone call and initial diagnosis. Now that I knew my problem was anemia, I thought about how I could bring more awareness to this condition, so that no one else would have to go through all the troubles I had experienced.

Later in the night as I tossed and turned, unable to fall asleep, I became nauseated. The pain subsided after three to five minutes. Thankfully, I was able to rest, and woke up the next day struggling to put my clothes on once more. With little to no energy to take a shower, I struggled to brush my teeth and wash my face. When transportation arrived to take us to the hospital, I could barely stand on my own. I needed the assistance of the gardener and house supervisor to make it out to the car. I was more fragile and weak than I had ever been. We took a trash bag because my nausea was still present. I began to vomit for what seemed to be the first fifteen minutes of the drive to the hospital. I became overwhelmed with embarrassment and feared that I would miss the bag and ruin the driver's car.

I was put into a wheelchair when we arrived at the hospital, and I remember feeling better as Toy registered my name for admission. My mind was a bit at ease and I relaxed somewhat, knowing I was in the hospital. I was taken to a room that held four beds, yet I was the only patient there. The hematology doctor came in and explained that I would be getting blood transfusions since my anemic level was so low. I was operating at 5.8 levels when the standard is 13.8, at the very least. This doctor was straightforward and took action immediately. I found comfort in this, mostly because the doctor appeared to be very knowledgeable and skilled in his profession as a hematologist.

Suddenly he said, "I looked more closely at your blood, and it appears you may have cancer in your blood."

Surprisingly, I remained calm. My arrogance got the best of me and the use of the word *"may"* comforted me in doubt. He told me I needed a bone marrow biopsy to confirm if it was indeed cancer. I still remember being calm, and when I looked at Toy, her face was without expression. I had no idea what she was thinking, but I was certain it was not relief.

The only reference I had to bone marrow at the time was from the movie *Seven Pounds* with the actor Will Smith. There was a scene in the movie where he decides to donate his bone marrow, and the expression on his face during the procedure was pure agony. Even still, the thought of this alone was not enough to bring me to my unfortunate reality. The doctor came back into the room about forty-five minutes later with an assistant, and they started the process of giving me a bone marrow biopsy. The only physical pain I remember were the two shots I took in my lower back and hip area. I could feel the aspirate needle used to twist out a tiny piece of my hipbone. My first thought after the numbing took place was how I could bring awareness to this sort of blood cancer once I was cured, because at this particular moment, this was my only thought. I truly did not know how to be fearful or nervous about the situation. Not only was my hipbone numb, but my emotions were numb as well. Then it hit me. The actual thought, it hit me like a ton of bricks—I could have *cancer* in my body.

Tears began to stream down my face as questions ran through my mind. "How am I going to tell my mother and father I have cancer?" "How am I going to tell my friends, especially my closest circle and my best friend, that I have cancer?" "What is Toy thinking, and how is she coping with the idea of me having cancer?"

The assistant noticed I was crying and she asked if the pain in my back was too much. I told her it wasn't the physical pain. I was breaking down emotionally. It hit me all at once, and the thoughts that I could have cancer terrified me.

When they were done with the biopsy, Toy and I sat in silence for at least ten minutes. She asked if I wanted to call my mother or father. I declined the offer. She encouraged me that we would get through it and she would be with me every step of the way. I felt selfish that my condition had caused and could continue to cause her suffering. Her life was about to change and it was because of me. Even to this day, she consistently reminds me—not only through her words, but through her actions—that she is with me throughout this entire process and beyond.

The doctor came back, and again without hesitation, he delivered the news that I had *cancer in my blood*. It was Acute Lymphoblastic Leukemia to be exact, a blood cancer referred to as ALL. He told me that this was now part of my life. Things happen to us that we never expect, but he assured me he would do everything in his power to get me into remission.

"There's a cure for everything!" he said.

My confidence increased greatly. He elaborated on things regarding the blood cancer. Most of it went in one ear and out the other as this shocking news overwhelmed me. Thankfully, Toy was there to write down as much information as possible. The doctor arranged for me to have X-rays done before the blood transfusions and then prescribed my new medications.

***

What can carry a person a very long way are words of faith, kindness and encouragement.

The transporter who escorted me to receive the X-rays was one of the kindest people I have ever met. He was genuine in trying to get to know me and my new diagnosis. I explained the situation the best I could, and he offered nothing but encouraging words. I remember one of the first statements he said after understanding my illness:

"Everything will be fine because we worship a truly amazing God, capable of all things. He shows us nothing but goodness and grace."

He told me that I was already taken care of, and God had already shown mercy and grace upon me. I listened, but I was still nervous about explaining everything to my mother, father and the rest of my family and friends. Never did the thought of "Why me?" cross my mind during this time, but neither did faith.

After the X-rays, the transporter bought me back to my room and walked out. He returned soon thereafter. He had a Bible with him this time and asked if he could share a few words with me. I agreed to his request, not knowing what to expect, but he had been very kind thus far. From his Bible, he read from the Book of Isaiah, chapter thirty-eight, *Hezekiah's Illness*. The scripture describes Hezekiah becoming ill to the point of death. The prophet Isaiah comes to him and tells him,

"This is what the Lord says: Put your house in order, because you are going to die; you will not recover." The scripture goes on to explain how Hezekiah faced the wall and prayed to the Lord.

"Remember, O Lord how I have walked before you faithfully and with wholehearted devotion and have done what is good in your eyes," Hezekiah said as he wept bitterly.

Then the word of the Lord came to Isaiah, and Hezekiah was told that the Lord had heard his prayers and seen his tears, and He would add fifteen years to his life. The Lord made the shadow cast by the sun go back the ten steps it had gone down on the stairway of Ahaz; this became the sign to Hezekiah of the Lord's promise to him. The transporter continued reading of Hezekiah's recovery in this same chapter, verse seventeen.

"Surely it was for my benefit that I suffered such anguish. In your love, you kept me from the pit of destruction." And in verse nineteen, the scripture says, "The living, the living…they praise you, as I am doing today; fathers tell their children about your faithfulness."

When this man finished reading to me, an indescribable emotion came over me. It truly spoke to me once I realized that ounce of faith I had asked for. I had asked for this faith when I had looked up at the sky, standing outside the classroom on my first day with the students. It started to take form when this caring man told me a story from his own life. He told me that when he was six years old, the doctors found an aliment with his heart, and he was given only a matter of months to a year to live out the rest of his life. He said he came from a faithful family and they had prayed to God to show mercy and grace upon his life.

"You know what, D?" he said to me.

I responded with a nod.

"Just last Friday, I celebrated my fortieth birthday! God is good, brother; you will be okay and He will see you through this situation."

In this moment, I truly recognized the power of prayer and having faith, even if it's only with a mustard seed. That's all you need to start to believe. This man changed my life, and ever since then, I have looked at cancer as a temporary pit stop to something greater to come.

Throughout my hospital stay in Cape Town, I received more kind words and encouragement that aided me in continuing to build my faith. Every nurse, administrator, medical technician and doctor that I encountered had nothing but wisdom and guidance to offer. Despite being ill, I soon began to feel better—first mentally, and soon thereafter physically, as a result of the spiritual growth I now experienced. I felt as if I had already been healed and the leukemia was out of my system. I really began to believe there was a higher purpose for my life, and being hospitalized would be exactly what I needed in order to refocus. On the fourth day of being in the hospital, I was discharged and sent back to the home-base. This was very exciting, as it affirmed my belief in a greater cause and purpose for my life. The power of prayer was in full effect, and God had truly placed his hands on me and would guide me through the rest of my battle with cancer.

*** ⸱

In the first couple of days back at the home-base, I began to read the Bible and tried to understand and incorporate its scriptures into my life. I repeatedly read the scripture that the transporter had given to me, as well as Psalms 23 and Proverbs 38. However, as the days went by, the voice inside of me kept telling me to go back and read the Book of Job in its entirety, without skimming through as I had always done. This voice told me to read and understand the messages being delivered in this story. Initially, after reading the first several chapters, old feelings resurfaced as I read about the turmoil and suffering of Job. I quickly reminded myself to complete the story and to not give into the old habit of not following through on my objectives in life. My objective here was to completely read the Book of Job with an open mind, and hopefully with an open heart.

One can easily side with Job in the beginning stages of his suffering. The question floated through my mind of why God, who was so powerful and merciful, would allow one of his own, who was upright and faithful, to be at the hands of Satan and his cruelty. Fortunately, I have learned that those who *believe* in the powers of God understand that the interruptions of life can devastate us, but they cannot kill our soul. Only our distrust can do that. With this acknowledgement, it should be understood that whatever attacks come our way, we have a choice to make. We can choose to fully believe and have courage in knowing that no matter the adversity, in the end we will still be well. Our soul will outlast any interruption that life has to offer, if we totally believe in a gracious and merciful God, whose powers are immeasurable beyond our comprehension. It even took Job a little while to remember that he serves a mighty God of omnipotent powers.

As I read more about Job, I began to notice sudden changes in my own perspective on life. Even though I was sympathetic to his situation, I couldn't help but to embrace my new outlook. First and foremost, I started to notice the wonderful spirit of the human being. The support from people continued to pour in, overwhelming me more and more with love. I pondered more sudden events taking place in my life; one in particular was the stack of homemade Get Well Soon cards that I received from the students I had taught at my first placement. My heart was full, and receiving those cards and reading their words was one of the most humbling moments I had ever experienced. The cards wished me well and a quick recovery. Some of the cards had messages hoping for a cure so I could come back and teach them, because they missed learning from me.

There were cards that addressed me as Teacher, Mr. D, DeAngelo and even De'Angel. I remember being at a loss for words when I first received the cards. I had tried to touch their lives in a way that would have a positive impact, and unknowingly they'd returned a greater favor by giving me more strength and courage to make it through my current situation. The heart is a mystery, but compassion, which the heart holds, is a powerful and undeniable love.

As Job continued to question all of the tragic events that had occurred in his life, I felt more sympathy for him. I continued to remind myself to finish the book before making any assessments. Not fully understanding the storm I was now in, things seem to be moving favorably in my direction with my treatment, especially toward reaching a stage of remission. Suddenly, another cloud cast upon the situation and soon the storm intensified. The travel agency insurance provider had asked the doctor to return me back to the States. I had only been out of the hospital for a couple of days, and according to the doctor, I was to go through a four-week plan of chemotherapy treatments before the first remission. At the time, if things were to go accordingly, it would then be safe for me travel twenty plus hours on a plane back home. The cloud got darker. The doctor advocated for me to stay in Cape Town and continue receiving the proper medical treatment, but the travel agency insurance insisted that I return immediately.

When it was all said and done, the travel agency insurance held the final decision even with the professional and medical expertise recommended from an accredited and proven doctor. Plans were made for Toy and I to travel in less than two days back to the States. I was determined not to leave Cape Town without the doctor's full assurance that it would be safe for me to travel. All was going well, despite the circumstances. The home-base staff was very accommodating with transportation and providing the proper dietary food I needed for recovery. Leaving at this point, when things seem to be turning in the right direction, was insane as far as I was concerned. With no other options available to him, the doctor took the necessary procedures to get me in the best health condition to travel back safely. He gave me blood transfusions and made sure I had plenty of fluids in my system to avoid dehydration. Toy had already made proper arrangements for me to get to the hospital upon our arrival. Everything was in place, and we began our journey back home.

I was advised not to consume any foods from the airport or on the plane because I was on a strict, low bacteria diet. Initially, I didn't think twice about this restriction, because I thought I would be fine with drinking protein shakes for the next twenty-four hours. I may have overestimated my ability to maintain in these circumstances a bit too much. After cutting our six-week volunteer trip to only four weeks, we arrived in Johannesburg from Cape Town on a layover. I was starving and had already consumed three protein shakes. My tastes for shakes were beginning to diminish quickly, and the sight of actual food wasn't making things any better. Toy was informed that baby food could help with my hunger, but I could not stomach the chicken-flavored mush and nearly gagged from the first spoonful.

We made it on the plane out of Johannesburg for Atlanta, Georgia, our final layover city before arriving in Columbus, Ohio. I was not only dehydrated and nauseated, but I looked it as well. The flight attendants were more than gracious, offering as much help as possible and assuring my comfort for the long flight. The other passengers around me didn't seem to be bothered by my condition, nor did most of the flight staff, except the lead flight attendant. She was gravely concerned and even made me a little nervous.

I was out of breath and very tired, which is why she may have been concerned, plus the facemask I wore, which made matters worse. Toy later told me that she was absolutely scared to death during this flight. Fortunately, once I took some sleeping pills, my nervousness wore down and I was able to observe our first class seats. The seats opened up, so I could prop up my legs and lay back comfortably. I was given plenty of blankets to stay warm, and extra pillows. The other flight attendants began to pass out glasses of champagne and strawberries. *Oh, the perks of flying first class!* I thought to myself. But before I knew it, I was sound asleep.

By the time we made it to Atlanta, hunger had taken on a new meaning. My vitals were extremely low, and I still couldn't eat solid foods. Our layover was three hours before the final flight.

***

The flight from Atlanta took less than two hours, but the delay appeared to go on for days as I felt every inch of my body yearn for nutrients and fluids. Toy arranged everything promptly for us to get transportation to the ER once we arrived home. A driver was waiting for us at baggage claim, and quickly but carefully drove us to The James at Wexner Medical Center at The Ohio State University. Unfortunately, we had to wait a couple of hours in the ER before I was sent back to the intensive care unit (ICU). I was still hungry, and a nurse helped to get me food. She brought back two cups of Chicken Noodle soup, and I felt like it was the best soup I had ever had. She also managed to get a plate of roasted vegetable lasagna, which was delicious and fulfilling.

As I finished eating, a medical team entered my ICU room. There were three of them, two oncologists and one nurse practitioner. They all wore white lab jackets and their demeanor came across as more conservative than my doctor and nurses in Cape Town. Toy had already spoken with the lead doctor on the team, but we still had to tell the story of how we ended up in the ER. They were quite amazed by our journey to South Africa and were empathic to the situation. One of the doctors began to speak about the initial information they had received from Cape Town regarding the type of cancer in my blood. This doctor painted a grimmer picture of my illness than the doctor in Cape Town. Perhaps it was the joyful spirit of the people in Cape Town that made me feel as if the battle with cancer had already been won. Their spirit had given me the peace of mind I had experienced up until this point.

Another nurse entered the room shortly after the doctors left, and informed me that I would be staying in the hospital for the next five to six weeks to continue my chemotherapy treatment. I was not too fond of this arrangement; however, when I got to the room I was told I could practically eat all the food I wanted with the exception of raw vegetables. This included fast food and comfort food, which was a relief, considering my mood was down and I was still very hungry. Toy went down to the cafeteria and got us burgers and fries. Afterward, I begged Toy to go home and get some rest. She had been remarkable throughout the entire journey, in addition to everything else she was doing for me. I could never repay her for all this kindness in the midst of disrupting her six-week dream trip to South Africa; my heart ached for her.

***

When Toy left, the night had fallen and I began to get settled into my new room. Unlike Cape Town, where the other three beds in the room became occupied with other patients, I was in this room by myself. The lighting was dim and the floor tiles were dark, which made the room appear to be even darker. I remember looking into the mirror in my room. For the first time since I had been diagnosed, I looked intently at my reflection and analyzed my facial hair, which had become dramatically different from what I had been accustomed to seeing. My mustache had grown thicker and wider. My eyes had sunk further into my eye sockets, and I noticed the dark circles around my eyes from the lack of sleep. My hair had stopped growing weeks ago and was thinning at the top. I thought it was just stress, because it happened so randomly. My hair didn't fall out completely; it just ceased to grow, even before my first dose of chemo. The natural brown color of my skin was fading, and I looked unrecognizably pale. I was unfamiliar with the person in the mirror, but I knew it was me—even with a slimmer, lighter face.

Right then and there, I said out loud, "Here we go, D!"

My phone rang as I sat in bed, searching for answers to questions I was unable to ask. It was my father, and hearing his voice was comforting, yet saddening at the same time. Even though I was back in the States, I still felt far from home. I could hear the concern in his voice as I explained my feelings to him. I was frustrated, because I felt as if I was moving in reverse regarding reaching remission. He told me no one, not even he, could understand the stress and confusion I was under, and there was nothing wrong with feeling the way I did. He also told me that I could not remain in this sort of mind set, and like many other obstacles in my life, I would overcome cancer. I remember my father encouraging me to use the "insight" within. At first thought, I didn't understand exactly what he was telling me. *Insight*, I thought. *What insight?*

He continued to explain that the "insight" is the wisdom and faith I needed to recognize that everything would be fine. Whatever knowledge and belief it took to get rid of my disease, he believed I would have the courage and willpower to see it through and that I wouldn't give up. This "insight" is something he had learned from me, his own son, and he had admired my ability to channel it. Honestly, I had never thought of myself in that way. Unknowingly, I suppose, I had just lived life, trying to handle what came my way the best I could. I knew my father was trying to make sure I maintained my mental strength more than anything. We had a good solid relationship, despite his absence earlier in my life. Over the past few years we had communicated and developed a very special bond. He had become of one of my best friends. But this was one of the few moments I truly became overwhelmed with the situation. My father continued to give me words of encouragement and let me know how I was loved by so many people.

I cried hard this time. Not just a couple of tears, but a lot. I cried so hard that I was losing breath and needed a couple cups of water to rehydrate. It was relieving and surreal to be able to express my feelings emotionally to another man and not feel less worthy. "Men don't cry" is what I've been schooled to believe my entire life. To cry or to show any emotion whatsoever is not a manly attribute. But when my father began to hear me cry, he didn't say, "Stop crying and man up." He simply said, "Good. Get that out of you. Let it out, son!"

He told me he knew all the frustrations and confusions I was experiencing were bottled inside of me. He had known for the past couple of months, even before the diagnosis, that I had been walking around like everything was well even though it was not. He had sensed it during the last few times we'd talked. I was embarking on a rite of passage unseen to my knowledge. Now that I think about it, most rites of passage are not known until we have taken a step back for a moment and reflect upon our particular experience. As I started to calm down, there was a moment of silence between my father and I. The last thing he said to me before we got off the phone was that I would be alright, and if anyone could get through this and come out on top, he had all the faith in me to make it happen. I felt a sense of relief, and my confidence to overcome the disease sparked once again. I couldn't have been more grateful for the conversation with my father.

My tears had run dry from my conversation that night, but I knew there was still more to let out. It happened while my nurses inserted IVs into both my arms. As tears streamed down my face, a nurse took notice. She asked if the needles were causing me any pain or discomfort and I told her no. I expressed my confusion as to why this was happening. More specifically, I told her since being in the hospital after returning from Cape Town, I felt like I was moving in reverse and not forward. I shook my head in doubt until she grabbed my hand and looked me in the eyes, giving me encouragement to make it through.

She told me this battle was more mental than physical, and I would need to maintain a strong mind in order to overcome. She again reminded me that it wouldn't be easy, yet not impossible; the doctors and nurses would be there to support me in any way imaginable throughout this recovery. She was sincere, and her confidence in my recovery reassured me that I would be fine. The conversation with my father and this particular nurse reignited my mental preparation for the next five to six weeks of my hospitalization. It was time for me to get back into battle.

PART FOUR: DEATH AND REBIRTH

During my hospital stay, I read more and gained new and different perspectives about life. The idea of death and coping with it definitely becomes a part of one's reality when treating a life-threatening illness. However, it wasn't until the second week of my six-week stay when I really began to think about and contemplate the idea of my own death. I was hopeful that I would get through this sickness and be cured of cancer. Yet to actually contemplate and put the idea of death into perspective was new to me. The first instance of analyzing the idea of death came from a YouTube video with Dr. Cornel West. He quoted Marcus Tullius Cicero, a Roman philosopher who said "That to study philosophy is nothing but to prepare one's self to die."

This statement threw me for a loop, but as I watched more, Dr. West continued to explain the intent behind such a bold and deep statement. The idea of death in this instance does not refer to the physical aspect of actually dying and being buried six feet under in a casket or through cremation of the body. This idea of dying is in regard to the spiritual being as you once knew it—or hadn't known it, for that matter. It is a spiritual dying and then being reborn. When you begin to study various philosophies about life, you are committing yourself to learning and developing a new way of living. Before I was diagnosed and even before my first hospital visits, I began studying philosophical books, essays and articles. When I started doing this, I had no idea I was actually beginning the dying process, which Cicero details.

For me, life was just giving me blank answers to the questions I asked. The more notable question, which everyone asks, is: "What is the meaning of life?" This question ultimately leads one to seek his or her purpose. I suppose another important question is, "How does one obtain happiness, and is such a thing truly possible in this life?" These were only a couple questions that were constantly on my mind; I was desperate to find answers.

I had spent so much time trying to leave no stone unturned that all I really wanted to do was accept what was happening in my life. I could never bring myself to accept the way things were, partially due to the demands I placed on myself, and the demands of trying to be successful. I read and researched ways to try to help me accept the things I could not control. I wanted a sure method of learning to live in the present moment and not dwell in the past.

Although trying not to plan for the future is a very difficult task, especially with an emphasis placed on preparation, there is a fine line between preparing for the future and predicting the future. Finding a balance between the two is where most of us, including myself, tend to be confused and drive ourselves to the brink of insanity.

As I laid in bed, staring at the dimly-colored walls and the dark green floor tiles of the hospital room, it dawned on me. I was in a casket. Obviously, I was not physically dead, but I imagined my own deathbed. For long periods of time, I would lie down and contemplate the idea of death. I completely read the essay by Michel de Montaigne, "That to Study Philosophy Is to Learn to Die." I must say that in the early stages of reading Montaigne's essay, it was chilling and frightening. He talks very openly about death. Further into the essay, I began to relax and also gain an appreciation about the unpopular topic.

With my increased appreciation for the knowledge gained from the Bible, there was no doubt that God's presence was around me and heavily influencing my walk of life. After the doctors expressed no idea of where my cancer originated, I took it as a sign and message. What I was going through was bigger than this disease; therefore, I needed to embrace cancer for what it was. In the Book of James,

Chapter One, verses two through four, it says, "Consider it pure joy, my brothers, whenever you face trials of many kinds, because you know that the testing of your faith develops perseverance. Perseverance must finish its work so that you may be mature and complete, not lacking anything."

***

"This is bigger than cancer!" I repeated to myself.

It was a statement I felt contained so much truth that it gave me the opportunity to gain even more knowledge about the journey of life and God's omnipotent powers. My faith grew stronger the deeper I got into the stories of the Bible and its concepts. The love of David for the Almighty taught me how to accept God as my ultimate source of power. My heart's conviction is that He is truly my rod and staff, and the table he prepares will only continue to elevate me higher to become one with God. The writings in Proverbs provided me with so much wisdom and a newfound outlook on life that at times I forgot where I was, in the hospital battling cancer. I began to walk down a new path in life, not by or for myself, but with and for Him.

As I began to understand and believe that death is a part of life, I questioned: Why do we fear it as much as we do? Even if someone would have told me, "D, in your book of life, there is a chapter where you will be diagnosed with cancer," I would have said, "Yeah, right!" and then laughed in their face. I admit I thought I was taking many of the appropriate steps to live a active lifestyle, like daily vitamin in-take, lifting weights, playing basketball and eating fruits and vegetables occasionally. I did things to keep my body as healthy and active as possible—I could have done better, but at least I was in the game, I thought.

Even though I had once contemplated taking my own life, I was one of those people who feared death. Driving in my car on the expressways in Chicago, I often wondered what would happen if one of the other vehicles on the road lost control and created a deadly collision of multiple cars. There were even times when I drove into certain neighborhoods, including the one I grew up in, and wondered if I would be mistaken for someone else, get robbed and killed all in the same instance. It would have been just my luck to get hit by a stray bullet. None of those things came true. I believe now that when it's your time to go, it's your time to go. There will be no "ifs" "ands," or "buts" about it. When death calls—and we all will be called—just have the faith in God's will.

There is a song by one of my favorite artists, Cee-Lo Green, titled "Gettin' Grown." Throughout the song, he speaks about his personal growth as a man, how he depends on God. There is one line, however—despite hearing the song over and over for several years—that never made sense to me until now. In the third and last verse of this song, Cee-Lo says, "And we all gotta earn to die." I previously had no reaction whenever I heard this line, other than that it rhymes with the rest of the song. However, one day while lying in bed at the hospital, I was listening to my iTunes and it shuffled to this very song. The line caught my attention so well that I listened to the song about five times in a row. "And we all gotta earn to die." As simple as this line was, the meaning of it brings forth so much wisdom that it's hard to avoid now.

As a Believer, it means to me that a person has accepted the charge of completing God's Will here on earth. The ultimate prize and goal of a Believer is to get to the Kingdom and carry out God's purpose. The Will of God is already written, but it takes much to carry out the Will assigned to you. First is acceptance, the acceptance that God is the Source. Next, it is the careful listening to your soul, which holds the messages from God that is for you, about the purpose assigned to you. Third, one has to embrace the purpose of God and know that whatever you're assigned with will be a heavy and difficult cross to bear, but you must. It shall be done. Joy, love, kindness, hope and most of all faith will come. Keep in my mind that great and precious things in life require hard work, which is why "We all gotta earn to die."

As Dr. West started my quest to understanding the concept of death, along with the readings of Montaigne, I soon became less fearful of dying in the flesh. My spiritual dying was coming to an end and a rebirth was beginning to take form within me. I no longer allow death or the idea of physically dying interrupt my daily routine. I simply do not have the time for it anymore. I truly believe that when it is my time, it's my time. I pray only that the purpose God has set forth for me will be completed.

***

Waiting for my lumbar puncture procedure, I sit on the edge of my bed and my room no longer appears to be a box, suffocating the life out of me. I sit staring out the window, watching the sky. Even though it is cloudy, I am not only grateful to be alive, but now I know the meaning of my life is to carry out my purpose from God. I may not always know exactly what my different charges are, but accepting and embracing faith is a good place to start.

I take a look at the bird soaring through the sky outside my window and I think of how amazing our Creator is, to be able to provide a creature that exudes such grace and peace. More so, I am honored to have been fortunate enough to be in its presence.

PART FIVE: GOD WORKS THROUGH HIS PEOPLE

Through reading and more deeply understanding the words and stories in the Bible, I began to notice one common theme: God works and comes to us in the form of people. Some years ago, I read the book *Celestine Prophecy* by James Redfield. Those familiar with this book will recall one of its key elements, that there are no such things as coincidences in life, especially when meeting someone new. There is always something to be gained during social contact with another individual. I am not talking about a quick glance between two people walking in opposite directions of each other—although something could be gained, like a kind smile. New contact between individuals in the book is taken as a way of learning new meanings to be used in the present time or future.

After reading the book, I attempted to learn something new from each person I met. I became conscious of those I newly met and the conversations we would share.

I incorporated the idea that God works through people delivering us the messages we seek. Such messages serve as confirmation to the questions and thoughts we have about life and our purpose. I have attempted each day to embrace this aspect as a way of life, and I have also realized there are events that happen to us beyond our understanding. We all hear stories and testimonies of people whose lives are affected by a supernatural force that could only be explained by the source of a miracle performed, and how people have overcome circumstances seemingly impossible for a human being. Again, there are no coincidences in life; my eyes were opened wider as I challenged myself to listen more effectively. We hear people talking all the time, but are we listening? Or have we grown accustomed to the sound?

Observing and giving more attention to the people I encountered on a daily basis became a start to paying more attention to the idea of no coincidences in life. All of the nurses, doctors and volunteers seemed to have a message for me, whether the message came through a long conversation or just a meet and greet. The family and friends who came to the hospital to visit or who called me by telephone suddenly felt closer than ever. I remember one Saturday night—there must have been at least ten family members and friends visiting me at the same time. We ordered food and I did not speak much at all. I was so appreciative and humbled by the people in the room. All of these people had taken time out of their schedules to spend an evening with me in the hospital. This kind of love was a new experience for me, and it was a very special night.

After six weeks of hospitalization, my health was now stable enough to be discharged without being in remission. I continued praying to God to give me courage and strength. Courage to maintain such newly found understandings of life, and strength to not become distracted in carrying out my purpose. I am convinced day in and day out that my personal advances in life do not matter anymore unless they help advance others. Change has to come, and during my stay in the hospital, I understood that change only occurs from within each individual; that is the reflection of a person's way of life.

There is still much to learn in this lifetime, even though I have learned a lot since my diagnosis. I have come to learn and accept that I do not have all the answers, or—to quote the great thinker Socrates—"I know one thing, that I know nothing." As each day allows me to evolve more and more, change is inevitable, since no two days are alike. Each day that I am granted to see the light of day is a clear reminder of the gift of life. The one certainty in this life, I believe, is there is indeed a God. The beauty of the sky, as well as the trees and the birds soaring above are just subtle reminders.

Life throws us many curveballs, which makes it very unpredictable. Whenever we put together a plan for our life, it typically never turns out exactly the way we expect it to. Things may happen along the way, but I have learned that you have to be willing to adjust. That is what my life has come to: reaction. As humans, we have been blessed with the ability to choose, and our choices are based off how we react to situations that occur in our life. Whether those situations are negative or positive, we have choices to make, and reactions are necessary. There is no denying this in any aspect of life.

Four months after I had been discharged from my six-week hospitalization, a nurse practitioner told me that the bone marrow transplant trial had been closed, and I did not become saddened by the news. Just three weeks prior, my younger sister decided to be my donor. My family and I were ecstatic. The chances of remaining in remission increases dramatically when a successful bone marrow transplant for an Acute Lymphoblastic Leukemia patient is conducted, especially if the donor is a blood-related family member. I remained at ease and tried not to think about death or my life ending soon. However, the action of not trying to think about something is really the act of thinking about it. Once I realized what I was doing, I immediately changed my thoughts to be more positive, like healthy lifestyle changes.

I committed myself to eating certain foods with the appropriate fibers and antioxidants to give my body more natural energy. I thought about practicing yoga, as well as meditations to help keep my body and mind at peace. Yet, the most important action I was not hesitant to do—and I started it even before the nurse practitioner left the room— was to close my eyes and pray. I prayed that God would continue to be my source of strength and power, since there is no other way of getting through this battle. I asked again for more guidance, more courage and more strength.

I prayed to God to give me the courage to walk the narrow path in life, where one's own agenda and preferences do not matter. What matters most is carrying out God's purpose, which we all have been tasked to complete. I prayed for the perseverance to push forward, despite the new obstacle of the bone marrow transplant trial being closed. As I prayed, I could feel the words from the Book of James: "Blessed is he who perseveres, because once he has stood the test he will be given the crown of life that God has promised."

CONCLUSION

I laughed just the other day at how I nearly jumped out the window of my hospital room—and, for that matter, out of my own skin—during a recent lumbar puncture procedure. The lumbar punctures had become a consistent part of my treatment. It was at least my fifteenth procedure to date, maybe more. I have honestly lost count. Anyhow, as the nurse practitioner was trying to the find the best spot in my spine to withdraw spinal fluid and inject chemotherapy, she accidently hit a nerve. A sharp pain ran down my left leg and up through the left side of my back and shoulder. My legs kicked forward and my spine felt like it wanted to burst through my chest. It was painful, but only for a couple of seconds. If I was not fully awake, then after my nerve was struck, I was definitely alert with eyes wide open.

After that, I felt myself becoming frustrated. For a moment I couldn't believe I was still going through this treatment. I thought to myself, *there must be a God somewhere*. It could have been the fact that I knew I would have to do the procedure in another month, or the fact that I was not scheduled for a bone marrow transplant. The idea of more chemotherapy crept into my thought process, and I was not too pleased by the idea. Suddenly, I remembered one of the greatest lessons I have learned during this entire process so far: life goes on. I shrugged my shoulders and laughed at how I'd nearly jumped out of my skin only a few moments before.

People often ask me how I continue to keep a steady head and a positive attitude in the midst of this battle with cancer. They say, "I don't know how you do it." I usually respond by telling them how I must press forward and continue to move on, because life will go on whether I am here or not. As life goes, I must too. It must be that way. By accepting this fact, I am not only able to move forward, but progress with a positive mindset as well.

I recall becoming confused and slightly disappointed when some family and friends were not checking in on me, since I had assumed they would, knowing I was battling for my life. Although there were many who remained in contact, there were those who I thought for sure would have been there and they were not. I went back and forth with myself about the reasons they were not keeping the lines of communication open.

But one day, as I sat on the sofa at home, I had a revelation. I realized those not in touch had a life of their own and the people who were staying in touch did as well. With the family and friends keeping in touch, I needed to be more thankful and appreciative that they made me a part of their lives. Instantly, I became aware I was lacking gratitude. Then I was grateful to those around, but mindful toward those who were not. They do not have an obligation to me, regardless of our previous and current relationships. People have their own families, jobs and lives. My condition should not make me so special that the world has to stop on my accord.

From this experience, I was able to learn the very fundamental and important lesson of life moving on. It is my understanding and acceptance of this truth that allows me to move forward, despite my battles. It allows me to maintain my faith and courage that God is with me; though at times I can not see His presence, I know He is with me. Whenever my departure from this world happens, the world will go on and everyone living in it will do the same. Faith assures me everything will be as it is meant to be.

***

On March 1, 2013, I received a Haplo Bone Marrow Transplant. My younger sister, a half-sibling, nineteen years old at the time, was my donor. I am grateful and blessed she agreed to become my donor. She is a small young woman in stature, but her heart is enormous. Her willingness to save my life is a noble act of courage, and no words could ever truly describe my gratitude. On October 13, 2013, Toy and I had a beautiful wedding with many loved ones in attendance. She continues to remain my rock.

Unfortunately, eighteen months after a successful transplant, I relapsed and the cancer returned. I had to be in the hospital while further tests were performed and a plan of action was determined. Within a day or two of relapsing, my father was hospitalized with bacterial pneumonia. To avoid additional stress on my family, I downplayed the severity of my relapse and disclosed very little information regarding my recovery process. My faith and confidence in the oncologists and medical staff to get me into remission again was my sole reasoning for considering my relapse of little importance. I was prepared for the recovery process and found solace in the outstanding medical advancements since my first diagnosis. In fact, my chemotherapy required no injections, just a small pill to be taken daily.

On January 6, 2015, as my recovery process got underway, I received an unfortunate and unexpected phone call. My father had succumbed to the complications of bacterial pneumonia and made his transition to the next life. I was completely heartbroken. However, in this moment, I was able to accept my father's untimely death and find a peaceful space. I found peace in knowing that in the last ten years we had worked hard to rebuild our relationship. My father had become one of my best friends. He was someone who I confided in and sought guidance from in trying times and situations. He played a vital role in being my support and encouragement during my battle with cancer. He often told me he was proud of the way I handled the diagnosis.

On many occasions, he expressed how I was his inspiration and role model. I was surprised when he expressed these sentiments, since I thought it was the other way around—the child admires the parent. I admired my father greatly. He had physical limitations and circumstantial setbacks, but he never crumble under the conditions. He put one foot forward and moved on, and did not allow himself to be deterred from living a full life.

I could always depend on a conversation with my father to discuss all aspects of life, from everyday struggles to the meaning of life. During each conversation, I was almost guaranteed to receive wisdom and knowledge that I could apply in my own life. Now that I was battling cancer again, I was without one of my most important advisors and confidants.

Through such despair, I channeled lessons from my father on persevering and accepting. He often reminded me to "Give time, time, son," and to "Get out of your own way." When he first expressed these sentiments they threw me for a loop, because I could not understand their applications to life. However, through meditation and contemplation, I was able to understand more clearly and gain a deeper appreciation for them as I got older. He was essentially encouraging me to be patient, to let go of things out of my control and to accept circumstances and situations for what they are and not what I wanted them to be. Most importantly, he often reminded me to allow God to work it out and to thank God for understanding.

My journey continues, and my life that includes cancer does as well, until a cure is discovered. But through this experience I found a true partner and soulmate in my wife, Toy. She and I walk this life together not only with faith in God, but also with faith in each other. This journey has transformed my beliefs into trusting the process and recognizing the beauty and wonder in every aspect of life, from the people I meet and see every day to the blue skies and the birds soaring above. I find true beauty lies in the pureness of life and not just in our own desires. I have learned that surrendering to life allows acceptance and life to unfold perfectly as it is. Each day presents a new opportunity to evolve and grow, for I am an infinite work in progress. By being open, free and present I have deepened my faith of the good to come.

Before I received chemotherapy treatment in Cape Town, I made a sperm deposit on the advice of the doctor. Toy and I are now hopeful that God and Cape Town will be good to us once again and work another miracle; this time to not only to save a life, but to welcome a new one!

THE END

ACKNOWLEDGEMENTS

It's with great purpose that I share my story, but also an obligation to those who have cared for and supported me throughout this journey. Each of these individuals is dear to my heart, and I love them with an infinite amount of sincerity. First and foremost, I am thankful and grateful to our Higher Source, whose light shines bright even in complete darkness. I am reminded to "Be Still" and "Let God." To my wife, Toy Lynn. There are no words that could ever describe the love, gratitude and appreciation I have for you. To this day, your love is constant and unconditional. The lengths you have gone and continue to go through, as my partner, can only be an act of God. I have many friends and family I am most grateful to have in my life. Our relationships and friendships continue to blossom, and I will continue to nurture them. All the physicians, nurses and health aides who have been there from the first diagnosis, to remission, and the back and forth from relapse to remission. Thank you for your constant help and guidance, and special thanks to my oncologist and psychiatrist. I would like to acknowledge and thank you all for your continuous support throughout my battle with cancer. To each of you I owe so much and to all those I pray may benefit from my story, I say thank you!